CATHERINE OF SIENA

by J. M. *Perrin*, O.P.

CATHERINE
OF SIENA

Translated by
PAUL BARRETT, O.F.M. Cap.

THE NEWMAN PRESS · 1965 · WESTMINSTER, MARYLAND

Originally published in French in 1961 by Aubier under the title, *Catherine de Sienne: Contemplative dans L'Action*, © 1961 by Editions Montaigne.

Nihil Obstat: Fr. Hilarius a Graigcullen, O.F.M. Cap.
                    Censor theol. deput.

Imprimi Potest: Fr. Conradus a Leap, O.F.M. Cap.
                    Min. Prov. Hib.
                    die 22 februarii, 1964

Nihil Obstat: Rev. Edmund J. Bradley
                    Censor Deputatus

Imprimatur: James Francis Cardinal McIntyre
                    Archbishop of Los Angeles

March 8, 1965

The *Nihil Obstat* and *Imprimatur* are official declarations that a book or pamphlet is free of doctrinal or moral error. No implication is contained therein that those who have granted the *Nihil Obstat* and *Imprimatur* agree with the contents, opinions, or statements expressed.

Library of Congress Catalog Card Number: 64-66333

Printed in the United States of America.

Acknowledgments

I SHOULD like to expess my gratitude to Very Reverend Father Hilary, O.F.M. Cap., Kilkenny, Ireland, for comparing my translation with the original and for suggesting improvements. I am indebted to Reverend Father Sadoc M. Bertucci, O.P., of Rome, for sending me the manuscript of his Italian translation of this book, which was invaluable in many ways. I am grateful also to Mrs. Frances Wylie Anderson, of Altadena, California, for typing my manuscript.

PAUL BARRETT, O.F.M. Cap.
La Canada, California

Contents

❖❖❖❖❖❖❖❖❖

CONTENTS

Part Three: THE APOSTOLIC LIFE

Part Four: THE CHURCH

Preface

SAINTS are our contemporaries in the Mystical Body, and through them Christ, who does everything in His Church, tells and gives us something of His plenitude. That is why, here more than anywhere else, we are interested only in the truth. Here mere legends or appealing fables are of no value when the reality of the past remains present and living as Christ fulfills and expresses Himself in the Mystical Body. The effort required to come face to face with a personality from another age and to penetrate the archaisms of an outmoded style is truly rewarding when it allows us to understand that exalted way of being a Christian and of living the Gospel in which sanctity consists.

We must acknowledge that in this matter we are more privileged than our predecessors. The learned and historical works of the past fifty years have profoundly changed our ideas of Catherine of Siena and her times. Furthermore, this new knowledge is now sufficiently well arranged to be at the disposal of non-specialists who simply wish to reflect objectively on her message. But we must also admit that in the light of these recent discoveries, Catherine's role in history has been diminished and reduced to less extraordinary proportions; yet, at the same time, our better knowledge of the age in which she lived throws her personality into greater relief and increases the significance of her message. Here, again, the truth is incomparably more beautiful than the legend, the more so because, due to Catherine's special vocation and her lack of merely human culture, her soul *was* her message.

We must admit, too, that a better knowledge of the archives of Avignon and Florence changes appreciably the hitherto current conception of her political career. Thus we find that Gregory XI was a greater, more far-seeing and more generous man than the usual biographies of Saint Catherine would lead us to suppose. He appears as a worthy successor to Urban V, although certain of his defects in connection with his family ties remain as evident as before. On the other hand, we learn that the Florentines were even more treacherous in their politics than was generally believed, and we can better understand how greatly Catherine was deceived in what was known as "the Avignon embassy." The Popes of Avignon themselves unceasingly desired and prepared for their return to Rome, so that we cannot say that Catherine took the initiative in this matter although she did do everything she could to hasten the fulfillment of her plan, employing to this end all her moral power, that power which was immeasurable and which, nevertheless, the archives scarcely mention.

These historical difficulties should not surprise us, because an account that concentrates on one person alone is in danger of making that person the center of everything and referring everything back to him either as the source of all things or as a standard by which they are to be judged. Hence comes the instinctive tendency to lean heavily on the law of contrasts and the inclination to belittle others in order to show the hero's virtues in greater relief.

Where sanctity is concerned, one's own personal idea of what holiness is can be fatal to the truth. Even when we do not go so far as to change the facts to suit our conception of what a saint should be, there is a danger that we shall first pick and choose our facts and then unconsciously interpret them to suit our ends. For example, if a hagiographer believes that sanctity consists principally in extraordinary mortification, revelations, visions and miracles, his attention will be caught by such things, and the greater the esteem he has for his saint, the more likely will he be to find them at the slightest hint. It must be admitted that Catherine's first biographers were of this type, although we cannot doubt the good faith of such of them as Blessed Raymond of Capua or Blessed Stefano Maconi.

In addition to all this, loyalty to one's group or religious order may come into play, and so, surprising though it may be, controversies have arisen about the relative merits of saints. It is shameful to recall, for example, that in Catherine's case, Franciscans and Dominicans quarrelled violently, as if God's graces were to be esteemed only because of their rarity or uniqueness, and as if the gifts which the Father bestowed on one of His children were not given for the joy and glory of the whole Church!

Finally, those hagiographers who are not themselves historians are content to repeat what their predecessors have said. That is what happens to all of us non-specialists when serious popular biographies do not place at our disposal the research done by historians.

Yet this does not mean to say that the present work is going to be a historical essay. On the contrary, we simply wish to examine Catherine's writings, and, by taking into consideration those works of hers that are available, ascertain her idea of the Christian life. Apparently, she held that the imitation of Christ is necessarily apostolic and that one's life must become a gift of love to God for His Church.

The problem of the influences that may have formed Catherine is of no interest to our purpose here. She was closely connected with the Dominicans, but, living as she did in the aftermath of the Black Plague, her level of culture was exceptionally low, as was that of the whole world at the time. She was also in close touch with the Augustinian current of thought, especially as it was represented by the hermits of Lecceto. Moreover, she could scarcely have avoided being influenced deeply by St. John Colombini, her compatriot who died when she was twenty and to whom her family was related. But all of that is of interest only to the history of spirituality.

On the other hand, however, we cannot study Catherine's personality and thought without examining in all their tragic reality the political situation in Siena and elsewhere during the fourteenth century, the violence of behavior and the general outlook that then prevailed. For that century was the era of the Black Death, the great Western Schism and the Hundred Years' War.

If this preface is to be an adequate introduction to our research, it must recall the situation of the Christian world in the fourteenth century and bring into proper focus the role of the extraordinary in every form of mysticism. We shall also explain the central idea of our research and, finally, indicate our sources of information.

*   *   *   *   *

Catherine was born in the very year that marked the beginning of the Black Death, that devastating plague which for two years was to ravage Europe from north to south, from Scandinavia to Sicily. Froissart estimates that "one third of

the world population died" of the plague; and in the margin
of a Dominican manuscript from Toulouse, we find a contemporary note to the effect that "this plague, which must
indeed be called great . . . , is such that no calamity like
it has been seen since the Flood."

Exact statistics of deaths are not available, especially because some cities were affected only slightly while others
were almost wiped out. But, nearly everywhere, the communities of mendicant friars were very severely stricken. For
example, the number of friars in the Dominican priory at
Montpellier fell, in one year, from 140 to 7; at Florence 78
friars died, and in Siena 50 of them succumbed.

These were terrifying losses, but even they were sur-
passed in later outbreaks of the plague. The Avignon district,
which had not suffered greatly in the first epidemic in 1348,
lost 17,000 people in the second outbreak in 1361. When
Catherine returned to her native city in 1374, she was confronted with another explosion of the plague, and we know
that, in all, she lost eight among her close relatives alone.

Taken by themselves these figures are appallingly eloquent,
but we would be poor judges of human nature if we regarded
this as the only evil wrought by the plague. Those who did
survive were panic-stricken, as we can gather from the poignant phrase of the Irish Franciscan, John Clyn, in a chronicle
that he began but was not to finish: *"inter mortuos mortem
expectans*—waiting for death among the dead." We also know
of Petrarch's sorrow when on one and the same day he learned
of the death of his friend, Cardinal Colonna, and of his beloved Laura. "Will posterity believe us?" he wrote later. "I
ask the historians, and they are silent. The physicians? They
remain sunk in a stupor. The philosophers shrug their shoulders, furrow their brows and put their finger to their lips to

enjoin silence. Yes, posterity will believe us, although we, who witnessed the disaster, find it hard to credit and think we are dreaming. To realize what has happened, one must have walked through the corpse-strewn streets and returned home to weep. O happy generation of our grandsons that will not know these evils!"

The effect of the plague on the poet's faith was not long in coming; from that year on, he began to lead a more religious life. But others whom death had spared gave themselves up to a frenzy of pleasure. As the Sienese chronicler Agnolo di Tura put it, "They live according to their whims." With some, fear distorted their religious outlook, and there was no lack of preachers to exploit their warped beliefs, with the result that flagellants and weird death dances began to appear on the scene.

In spite of the warnings of General Chapters, beginning with that of the Dominicans in Lyons in 1348, the religious orders only too often accepted badly prepared candidates to fill up the empty places in the communities. As a case in point, the General Chapter of the Dominicans, held in 1376, referred to Dominican students who did not know how to write! The Chapter spoke reprovingly, of course, but the mere mention of such things is indeed significant.

The appalling losses suffered by the mendicant orders in the middle of the fourteenth century shook the very foundations of the religious life and destroyed some traditions forever.[1]

When we examine the political situation more closely, in Siena particularly, we are struck by the violence and instability

[1] "It is impossible that such a depletion should not have affected the mendicant orders' later mode of life and that it should not have been responsible for changing their aims in the future" (LeFebvre, *Annales*, 1949, p. 102, note).

that prevailed. Dante had said that the Sienese were the most fickle of men, by far surpassing in this respect even the French; and after the plague their habits of violence were even worse than those which the poet had known. There was nothing but revolutions and counter-revolutions, coalitions between factions and pitiless betrayal. Catherine's family belonged to the *popolo minuto*, the party of the lower classes, which took an active part in these upheavals. They were to escape massacre only by a miracle, and a little later extricated themselves from a similar danger by paying a very heavy fine.

In giving these details, we are not arbitrarily selecting somber colors in order to paint a dark picture of the fourteenth century. Instead, we are only recalling to mind some facts to describe the historical context in which Catherine played her part.

In the world at large the political situation was no more stable than in Siena. From outside the Christian world, the Moslems were pressing so hard that the collapse of the Byzantine Empire and the fall of Constantinople, which were to occur during the course of the next century, could already be foreseen. This Moslem offensive was not to be broken on the seas until the battle of Lepanto in 1571 and on land until the battle of Vienna in 1683. Within the Christian world, besides less lengthy conflicts, the Hundred Years' War broke out, setting the strongest forces of the West at each other's throats for a century. For many nations the times of peace were as full of menace and evil as the years of hostility. The "great companies," which made a business of war by hiring themselves out to the highest bidder among the belligerents, lived off the country and withdrew only when paid a large ransom.

The world of business, shaken by terrible famines and by

the consequences of the Black Death, was greatly affected by a profound change in communications.

As regards the general mentality of the age, the faith of the Church, thanks to the revolution in preaching which the creation of the mendicant orders in the thirteenth century had brought about, had conquered heresy for the most part, although embers still smoldered beneath the ashes, ready to burst into flame at the propitious moment. The "Spirituals," who combined the best as well as the worst features of religious fervor with unparalleled violence, and who called into question the authority of the Church and the State, were everywhere. Pope John XXII had dealt severely with them but had not succeeded in suppressing them, and the ideas that they proclaimed continued to circulate.

As a result of these upheavals, revolutions and wars, the situation in Italy was so unstable that the Sovereign Pontiffs preferred to establish the Papal See at Avignon. This state of affairs and the predominant feeling were to open the way for the schism in which the cardinals, angered at the defects of the Pope whom they had just elected in Rome, elected another "Pope," who, after several months, would take up his abode in Avignon, while the legitimate successor of St. Peter remained in Rome. The Christian world, confused and torn apart, did not know what to think and became divided between the two claimants to the papal throne. This brings us to Catherine's lifetime; in fact, to the last years of her life.

Undoubtedly this was the most harrowing trial the Church has ever gone through, although neither the Faith itself was in question nor the certitude that Christ had founded His Church on Peter. Instead, the whole issue was simply to determine who exactly was St. Peter's successor. As we look back over the centuries, we can see how this time of trial was to make men much more keenly aware of Catholic unity and of the spiritual cohesion necessary for the Church. But in the four-teenth century, the Christian world felt only the piercing reality of the disaster.

Catherine's intrepid, joyous faith, her inexhaustible energy, and her insatiable and selfless yearnings will stand out in high relief against the circumstances of her life. The anguish of the world in which she lived, the difficulties she met with, the prevailing outlook against which she had to react—all help us to understand better the apostolic inspiration of her life and the significance for her of the words which she heard spoken within her: "I wish to show mercy to the world. . . . My servants are the remedy. . . . I wish to show mercy to the world through My servants."

From these words we can gather that Catherine simply wished to be an echo of God, and also that revelations, visions and other extraordinary manifestations played an important part in her consciousness and in the formulation of her message.

* * * * *

Not only is the whole of Catherine's life filled with ecstasies and visions, but she presents nearly all her teachings as having been received directly from God. Almost all of the *Dialogue*, which is her testament and the summary of her mystical experiences, is spoken by God in the first person. However, we can easily demonstrate that such expressions are far removed from the general outlook in our day and are for us a source of suspicion rather than of credence.

Therefore, when we refer to the doctrine found in the *Dialogue* or in the revelations in which Catherine expressed herself, we are not seeking any new revealed teaching but only the manner in which the Holy Spirit, through her, "brings

to our minds" Christ's words. We shall not concern ourselves
with the mystical problem but shall only endeavor to ascertain
her conception of the Gospel ideal and the manner in which
she, animated by the Holy Spirit, perceived and passed on to
us the divine realities.

When she sees the heavens darkened with demons; when
she is dazzled by the beauty of the soul created in the image
of God; when, on the threshold of eternal happiness, the soul
of Nicola di Tuldo thanks her with the graciousness of a bride
entering the nuptial chamber, it would be altogether too naive
of us to think that Catherine or her correspondent, Fra Raymond, forgot for one second that they were dealing with
spiritual things which are as totally beyond the grasp of the
imagination as they are outside the range of our five senses.
This is only Catherine's and Raymond's way of perceiving
and describing a supra-sensible reality.

We can, perhaps, find a parallel in the world of esthetics.
The same atmosphere of farewell that pervades an autumn
landscape will be expressed by one romantic poet as a lan-
guorous song, and by another as a *Magnificat* for peace after
fruition. An impressionist will paint such an autumnal scene
as a remote countryside, while an abstractionist will depict
it in some unusual form, and a musician will interpret it as a
melody. Hence we are not interested in the fact that a mystic
with an imaginative style of writing will clothe his experience
in a visual or auditory form. We shall merely try to ascertain
from his experience how one and the same Spirit who built
the Church expresses Himself in that mystic. Furthermore,
recalling Christ's promise, we shall ask ourselves which of His
words the Spirit wishes to "bring to our mind" (see John
14:26). In short, we shall concern ourselves only with that
which is eternal and universal.

For example, St. Catherine reported the words which she

heard God addressing to her, urging her to cooperate in the mercy which He willed to show the world. Later, St. Teresa was to give admirable expression to the immense desires she felt surging and growing within her. Again, a Catholic Actionist noted in her diary: "At Communion I understood better what I must carry out into the streets and the workshop —the love of Christ that I am receiving." Or, as another one concluded at the end of her retreat, "Since Christ so loves me, I want to lead the young people of my village to Him."

In each of these cases, it is the same Holy Spirit who brings to mind the words of Christ asking that our Father's kingdom may come and that the Gospel be preached "to every creature."

Those who are fond of the extraordinary in spiritual matters are in great danger of becoming engrossed in psychological phenomena and may not relate them back to the divine reality of which they are a human, although miraculous, expression. These persons may also isolate such phenomena from the universal life of the Church. But we average Catholics run an even greater risk—namely, that of being contented with our mediocrity and of not increasing our efforts and our desires in order to adjust them to the Truth; the risk of being satisfied with ourselves instead of really striving to follow the logic of the Faith by abandoning ourselves to the Holy Spirit, whose action is infinitely more intimate and more marvellous than any revelation can express.

Our main interest in this study is St. Catherine's interior vision, which furnishes us with an occasion for hearing once more our Lord's own words, for her vision is a new, although imperfect, expression of the Faith that we hold in common, of the unparalleled words of Christ, preserved and re-uttered by the Church in the fourteenth as well as in the twentieth century.

Catherine was not unaware that there is no comparison between the most extraordinary graces given while we are on earth and the face-to-face vision of God:

> "Every vision that the soul receives while it is in this mortal body is only a shadow when compared with the vision that the soul enjoys when separated from the body."
>
> (*Dialogue*, Chap. 79.)

And when writing to one of her close friends, she used the expression "Thus the mouth of Truth seemed to say" (Letter 70, to Fra Bartolomeo Dominici), from which we can gather that she realized the chasm that existed between her own words and the mystery of God. But there is no reason why this chasm should deprive us of the beautiful image which we find in this letter and which reminds us that God is love and that we have come from that love: "I am the fire, and you are the sparks."

A detail which had to be verified in the original manuscript is quite significant on this point. In the *Dialogue*, God puts on the lips of "His glorious Apostle Paul" a phrase which is not St. Paul's but which, instead, belongs to a later Christian tradition. What, then, are we to think? First, we can conclude that Catherine's secretaries and Blessed Raymond himself were scrupulously honest, seeing that they did not correct such a glaring mistake. Next, and especially, we see that God's enlightening action uses man's images and knowledge, his concepts, language and words. In all of this, what interests us is the divine thought that must enlighten man and re-state for him in his own fashion the common doctrine confided to the Church.

We must make one final remark about revelations and prophecies—a remark suggested by the story of Jonas as re-

lated in the Bible, which does not lie. You will remember how
the story goes. The prophet does all he can to evade the mission which he feels that God has entrusted to him. He foresees
that God, who is merciful, will not carry out the threats that
he must announce, and, in fact, this is what happens. Niniveh
repents and is spared. The intention which God manifested
prophetically here was, perhaps, conditional, depending upon
men's reaction, since penance can avert the carrying out of a
threat, while, on the other hand, infidelity can prevent the
fulfillment of a promise. This was Catherine's thought upon
a similar occasion. Christ had commanded her to preach peace
to the Florentines, a command that had filled her heart with
joy. But two years later, although the city was once more
restored to peace and reconciled with the Pope, it was still
in the grip of such fearsome passions and cruel resentments
that Catherine had to depart in secret, sadly comparing her
former joy with her present bitter disappointment.

We do not refer to these incidents because we are particularly concerned with conditional prophecies, for we intend
to pursue our study from a completely different point of
view. However, it is interesting to note in passing this added
difficulty in the study of prophecies.

In the first century and in the fourteenth, and even today,
after all the progress that has been made in psychological
studies, the only valid criteria of mystical phenomena are the
fruits they bring forth in the soul. Here the words of the
Gospel are applicable in all their rigor: "By their fruits you
shall know them." And modern psychology agrees, for it, too,
wants to know whether the inner life of the soul progresses in
unity and truth, in closest contact with objective reality. Thus
we must ask whether the strength acquired or the impetus
given is enriched by its complementary virtue. Are uprightness
and understanding, zeal and mercy, chastity and cordiality,

firmness and gentleness, spontaneity and maturity combined in an interior synthesis that is both rich and apparent?

When the Church examines a candidate for canonization, she inquires into the high degree of his virtues, or, as it is called in technical language, "the heroicity of virtues." That is what the Church acknowledged in canonizing Catherine, whose heroic virtues are readily apparent when we study with loving attention her incredibly rich personality, glowing with health and enthusiasm, radiating joy and strength in the midst of her increasing infirmities and her unusual graces.

* * * * *

In Catherine's altogether extraordinary life, the only elements that interest us are those which she had in common with the Gospel and the Faith of our baptism. When we were dealing with the historical background of her times, we were intent simply on grasping what was timeless, universal and applicable to ourselves therein. So, too, here we are seeking, not the exceptional, but only the essential.

When we thus go beyond the accidental circumstances of her life, we are attracted by her personality; we find that, although she was only a young girl, her spiritual insight, her joy and vitality were most engaging, and that her generosity, energy and forgetfulness of self were not only outstanding but also utterly charming. In particular, we find that her soul *was* her message, so that she did not have to speak of herself but merely expressed her inner vision in all things, referring everything back to Christ alone.

She was truly a miracle living in the midst of the world, fighting the evil that she continually encountered there. She experienced the opposition of the declared enemies of the Gospel and of those who quoted it as their credentials, of those whom Blessed Raymond forcefully named "the satraps of the Philistines," and whom Catherine, in her usual down-to-earth way, called "devils incarnate," "devils and she-devils." She addressed herself to people who lacked all prudence, who had lost heart, who were overburdened with temporal cares, who had forgotten what the Church and its message meant, who had no perseverance and courage, who were swamped by their passions, or who grew weak in the face of adversity. When she spoke about her neighbor and the Church, or about the world's sins and salvation, she did not do so like someone from another planet. The advice that she gave goes right to the point and, though the form in which she expressed it may seem to us unusual or perhaps antiquated and outmoded, with a little effort we can find in her words a re-statement of the essentials of our Christian life.

It is of small importance to us to learn that historians can point out the influences that worked upon her, that learned men can detract from her originality by showing that such and such an expression of hers was not her own creation. We are not concerned with such things, but only with the vision of love which she received while communing with Christ and which made her one of the most effective co-workers in the Redemption, one of those souls who, in living their faith to the full, are able to combine the closest union with Christ and the most effective action in His service. She became an apostle because of the logic of her faith and the genuineness of her love. There is no doubt that this is what marks her off from the rest of the Catholic mystics, the majority of whom had a vocation and followed a form of life that withdrew them from the world or at least confined them to one particular sphere of action. This is what makes her a contemporary and a sister to all those who live out their baptismal obligations in circumstances similar to hers.

For that reason we shall let Catherine speak freely for herself; her own words are the best introduction for us to that interior world which she bore about with her.

When we take pains to understand her and to grasp the meaning behind her words—unfortunately available to us only in translation—we shall see that her message is truly universal. Because she did not receive any formal education, her roots sprang straight from the common teaching of the Church, from that direct experience and ardent love which allowed her to drink from the very source of wisdom. We could speak of her genius, but we should rather speak of her inspiration, which she received in the secrecy of her heart. Her doctrine is all the more capable of being shared and communicated because so much of it is simply the light of faith reflected by the intellect. Some have mentioned Catherine's "intellectualism," in a certain sense. However, that is rather a lofty term to express the fact that she used her mind enthusiastically. Her divine Teacher ceaselessly urged her "to open the eye of her intelligence," and she in turn never tired of employing the same words to petition her correspondents to reflect attentively. But to see intellectualism in this would be to forget that she was simply using her common sense in considering the truths of the Faith. It is true that she did appeal untiringly for reflection, for close attention, but not more than was demanded by God's injunction to "listen." Her message contained the kernel of the Faith, which it repeated in human words and which must be assimilated in the spirit of reflective attention that she enjoined.

It is thus that we shall learn from her how the love and imitation of Christ become apostolic sanctity.

* * * * *

To help us in our inquiry into the ideal of sanctity that attracted Catherine, the interior vision that guided her efforts, and the concept she formed of the meaning of life in Christ, we have first of all her *Dialogue*, a mature work in which she summarized her experiences so that she could leave them as a spiritual testament to her friends and disciples. When she dictated the *Dialogue* in October 1378, ten years had passed since she had left her self-chosen cell to work for the salvation of the world. She was thirty-one years of age and had only a year and a half to live.

We cannot exaggerate the worth of this book, although the form it takes may discourage us somewhat and although we will have to make an effort to assimilate the teaching it contains. Not only is it a mature work, in which Catherine sets down in one place all the themes that enlightened her throughout her life and filled her correspondence; it is also a confrontation between Catherine's piercing anguish at the evils that beset the Church, a confrontation between her anguish and Him who wished to show mercy to the world through His servants.

Besides the *Dialogue*, we have twenty-six prayers, taken down by one or other of Catherine's secretaries as she prayed aloud in ecstasy. Then there are the numerous letters which she dictated to her secretaries and of which three hundred and eighty-two have been preserved. These letters possess a vigor and spontaneity that could not be counterfeited, although they do pose many problems of chronology that make it impossible to date them or to determine the sequence in which they were written. They are more her spoken than her written words; in fact, they are her soul expressed in her own words. Of the majority of them it is true to say that "the more a word resembles a thought, the more a thought resembles a soul, and the more a soul resembles God, the more beautiful it is." The letters were addressed to all kinds of people—some to Pope Gregory XI and some to Urban VI, others to religious communities, to anonymous persons, and even to a prostitute—that is, to people striving for sanctity as well as to sinners. Some of them deal with important civic matters and the affairs of the Church, while others overflow with love or answer a specific question. Almost always the themes are the same as those of the *Dialogue*, but are treated more directly and spontaneously although usually less completely than in the *Dialogue*.

Out of all this voluminous correspondence, there is one letter that is incomparable for its transparent sincerity, its affection and trust—the one that Catherine wrote to "the father of [her] soul," to "the very dear father given [her] by gentle Mary," as she liked to repeat. Rarely have souls been united by bonds of friendship stronger than those that existed between Catherine and her "dear father," Blessed Raymond of Capua. Although she did reproach him for his lack of courage, referring to "the milk teeth" that he retained so that he was "unable to chew the tribulations that are the food of the strong," and although, very often, the tone of her letters to him was more that of "a mother than a daughter,"[2] it would be wrong to see only this aspect of the matter. As we said, Catherine loved to repeat that Blessed Raymond had been given to her by our Lady to help her in her spiritual ascent and especially to bring her the light of a doctrine that was

---

[2] We must not forget that these letters of Catherine's to Raymond, as well as the other letters, have been handed down to us by the recipients and that, most of the time, occasional details and circumstantial allusions deemed of no interest have been deleted. Hence they have been shorn of all that might appear too personal, which was passed over in discreet silence, as sometimes happened also with expressions that might appear unsuited to the glory of a saint or simply to the memory of a deceased friend. It has been pointed out, too, that in some of Catherine's letters a series of personal allusions, requests and messages are found at the end of the letter, following the "spiritual" part.

soundly based and broad in scope. She did not hide the fact that she lacked help when "the gardener was not there to remove the thorns from the garden," or that in her greatest struggles she was deprived of the assistance which "the father of [her] soul" gave her. Indeed, she declared that she was always united to him in spirit when she stood before God. To prove our point, let us read the concluding sentences of her last letter to Raymond, in which, having a presentiment that her death was very near and yet being uncertain of God's designs, she took her leave of him:

And please forgive me all the disobedience, irreverence, ingratitude, pain and distress for which I was responsible in your regard, as well as my lack of zeal for the salvation of us both. . . . Your presence would have been a very great consolation to me, but to see that you are bearing fruit in Holy Church consoles me much more and fills me with joy.

(Letter 373.)

In addition, she called him "St. John," and there is no need for us to stress the love and respectful confidence implied by her choice of name.

Nevertheless, as we gather from her own words, Catherine was separated from Raymond at the most important moments of her life. He preceded her to Avignon, and later she wrote to him from Florence—a correspondence from which we learn her thoughts during the first great Florentine crisis. He was in Rome when she returned to Siena, and from her letters to him there we know what her reactions were when Gregory XI was thinking of repudiating her. And when Gregory sent her once more to Florence, Raymond was again in Rome. But, worst of all, only a few days after Catherine's arrival in Rome, Urban VI decided to entrust to Raymond some very important tasks, particularly the project of sending an embassy to France in order to avert King Charles V from schism. Because of these separations and the resultant correspondence between Catherine and Raymond, we are allowed to glimpse the vision that filled her soul in her most heroic moments, and it is to this correspondence also that we owe some of the most beautiful passages ever written on love for the Church.

Then there are the confidences which she made orally to those close to her, the first of whom was the same Raymond, who was also the author of the *Life* or *Legenda Major*—a "legend," not in the modern sense of a fable, but in the Latin sense of something that should be read, just as we still speak about the "legend" on a map or a painting when we mean an inscription that provides necessary information. Not only did Raymond know Catherine better than anyone else, but he was also able to interrogate every member of her spiritual "family," from her mother, who survived her, to her former confessors and the tertiaries who had been associated with her and who had always been on the lookout for the smallest edifying detail in their spiritual sister's life. Moreover, Raymond solemnly testifies that his account is an accurate one, and he never omits telling us how or through whom he learned what he is describing.

Therefore, the life of St. Catherine written by Blessed Raymond of Capua is an invaluable source of information about her. In it, Raymond, whose qualities were so outstanding that his fellow Dominicans later elected him Master General of the Order, speaks to us out of his intimate knowledge of the Saint, gained by untiring cross-examination of witnesses and scrupulous verification of facts.

Despite this, we must admit that the modern reader of Raymond's book feels a growing disappointment because, as he reads, he becomes increasingly aware that there has been a misunderstanding somewhere, that there is a widening gulf between what the author presents and the reader's expectations. Raymond is less intent on writing about Catherine and her part in history than he is on presenting her credentials for canonization. He talks of miracles, visions and prophecies with obvious sincerity and without the slightest awareness of the problems which such phenomena present for anyone with a scientific cast of mind and a knowledge of psychology.

Nevertheless, despite the modern reader's disappointment and the radical difference between his and the author's points of view, Catherine's life story is still a rich source of information. Her personality emerges clearly from Raymond's allusions and from first-hand observations—a singularly attractive personality, alive with joy and a wondrous forgetfulness of self. Raymond uses the words *joy* and *happiness* repeatedly, and often mentions Catherine's smile that captivated those who met her. As regards the visions and the extraordinary events which he records, we shall strive to discover in them Catherine's thoughts and outlook; we shall seek to know her mind by examining the things she saw in her visions.

Other authors who were very close to her, although not as close as Raymond, have also left us accounts of her life with which they, too, had been directly connected. Such was Tommaseo Caffarini, who wrote the *Leggenda minore* and whose objectivity often seems to be overcome by his admiration for Catherine and his desire to extol the spiritual family to which both he and she belonged. However, Stefano Maconi's account avoids these faults despite the great affection apparent in it. Of the various depositions taken during the process in Venice, Stefano's is one of the most delightful because of its charm and the spirit that inspired it. This process, opened in Venice in 1411 to gather information for the Pope about the life, virtues and miracles of Catherine, the Servant of God, is an indispensable source of material on her. Despite the very precise point of view from which such inquiries are always conducted and despite the fact that they are not usually begun until many years after the person's death, these processes are a veritable mine of information for the historian.

Finally, Catherine lived in an age when all sorts of things were faithfully entered in records. Our interest is aroused therefore when we find an entry in the accounts of the papal treasury at Avignon, dated September 12, recording a special gift of a hundred florins to Catherine for her travelling and living expenses, the money to be given to Fra Raymond for her. Again, in the minutes of the council of Siena, we find that when Catherine sought permission to build a convent on the ruins of a former castle-fortress, 333 members voted "yes" and 65 voted "no." Finally, a Sienese ambassador to Rome, writing on November 30, 1378, to inform the republic of Catherine's arrival in Rome and the very favorable reception accorded her by Pope Urban VI, said:

Catherine, daughter of Monna Lapa, has come here, and our Lord the Pope has seen and heard her very willingly. No one knows anything about what he has asked of her. All we know is that he saw her willingly. . . .

Nevertheless our curiosity remains unsatisfied because records such as these tell us almost nothing about the private opinions and intentions of the dignitaries they mention.

But, even more, the parts that interest us most have no special claim to authority since, as far as Catherine is concerned, the documents themselves are not official, a fact which lessens their historical importance for us and inclines us to view their references to her as mere imponderable private opinions.

Moreover, it is obvious that such documents and their

interpretation are the province of learned men, and that real historical competence is required to use them properly. We are indebted, therefore, to research workers in history and to those who pass on to us their erudition and hard-won discoveries, for thus we who are not expert historians can come into contact with the real Catherine. For example, when we know the date of a letter or the circumstances in which a certain document was written, we can obtain a better insight into the meaning of the words and thereby get a glimpse of the Saint's mind.

Thanks to these documents and to the works that make them available to us, we can, as it were, ask questions of Catherine herself, and from her own words learn about her love, her ideals, her concept of the Christian life and her vision of the universe. That is why it is best, as far as is possible, to let her speak for herself and to have recourse to the very words in which she expressed her thoughts, even though we must be content with reading them in translation instead of in her own vivid Italian.

As we have said, what interests us in her is, not what she did or said in the far-off fourteenth century, but what she *was* and what she can teach us about the way in which she viewed the Gospel and put it into practice. We are not concerned with the past but with that which is timeless or, rather, with that which is present and actual, the elements in her life and character that we can incorporate into our own.

In accordance with this central idea, we shall devote the first part of the book, not to re-telling her life, but to understanding the spirit and the intentions that inspired her diverse activities. In other words, we shall seek to depict her personality.

Catherine's life was an apostolic one spent in the midst of the world, and this was the concept that she wished to share with and impart to others. In her eyes, everything came down to realizing the ideal which she expressed to herself in the following words: "To become to Him like another self through a union of love" for the glory of God in the salvation of souls.

The references throughout are to the following editions (all, except the *Life,* are after S. M. Bertucci, O.P.):

Dialogue: *Dialogo della Divina Provvidenza,* ed. by P. Innocenzo Taurisano, O.P., 2 vols., Florence, Libreria Editrice Fiorentina, 1928

Fioretti: *Fioretti di S. Caterina da Siena,* ed. by P. Innocenzo Taurisano, O.P., second edition, Rome, Ferrari, 1927

Leggenda minore: *Leggenda minore di S. Caterina da Siena,* ed. by F. Grotanelli, Bologna, 1868

Letters: *Lettere di S. Caterina da Siena,* with notes by P. Lodovico Ferretti, O.P., 5 vols., Siena, 1918

Life: *The Life of St. Catherine of Siena* by B. Raymond of Capua, trans. by George Lamb, New York, P. J. Kenedy, 1960

Prayers: *Orazioni di S. Caterina da Siena* in *Le Opere di S. Caterina da Siena,* ed. by Antonio Ansano, Rome, 1868, after the edition by Girolamo Gigli, Vol. 3

Supplemento: *Supplemento alla Leggenda del B. Raimondo da Capua,* by Fra Tommaseo Caffarini, trans. by P. Ansano Tantucci, ed. by Antonio Caioni, Rome, 1866, after the edition by Girolamo Gigli, Vol. 2

Part 1. *Vocation*

❖❖❖❖❖❖❖❖❖

Part I. Vocation

1. Divine Preparations

CHRIST lives in each of the members of His Mystical Body, whence comes their diversity, each being simply a minute reflection of His plenitude; and thence comes also their unity, since He alone does everything in all of them. To Catherine it was granted to share in God's loving will to save men by incorporating them into His Body, which is the Church. That was the great discovery of her life, a discovery that was to become her message to the world.

It will not be necessary for our purpose here to relate in detail the external circumstances of her life but only to recall its general outlines so that we may understand the thoughts and motives that guided and inspired her. Accordingly, we shall study in turn the way in which God prepared her, her personal apostolate, her mission in the Church, and her self-oblation for the Church—all of which are inseparably related to each other in the unfolding of her life. Her personal, direct apostolate to individuals did not cease when she was engaged in public affairs; on the contrary, it was then that she reached the zenith of her influence on individuals, and, even when she lay on her deathbed, she kept on fighting the schism that rent the Church. For the rest, when we are reading her life we must never forget that barely thirteen years elapsed between

3

her emergence from solitude at about the age of twenty and her death on April 29, 1380.

She was born in Siena on March 25, 1347, the twenty-third of the twenty-five children of Giacomo Benincasa and his wife, Lapa. Giacomo was a dyer and, although he was relatively well-to-do, he belonged to the *popolo minuto*, the lower classes that were acquiring more and more influence in the Italian cities.

Catherine was a well-behaved child, strikingly graceful and very pious. Later she was to tell her confessor that whenever she went upstairs she used to delight in saying a Hail Mary on each step. When she was about six years old, she had a vision as she was walking along the street. She saw Christ dressed in pontifical robes, wearing the tiara, and smiling upon her with infinite tenderness—a vision which left her with an impression of love, beauty and majesty, as we learn from the same confessor, who had the account from Catherine herself. It is no wonder, then, that she was completely given to God in a gift of self which she confirmed by taking a vow of virginity.

She longed to imitate the saints and, in particular, felt an instinctive affinity with St. Dominic. Moreover, she had such respect for the apostolic vocation that she often devised excuses for kissing the pavement on which one of the Dominican friars from the neighboring priory had just trodden. She herself wanted to become a Dominican *friar*, a dream inspired by the legend of St. Euphrosyne.[1]

At the age of twelve, Catherine was a strong, healthy girl, able to lift a donkey-load of material and carry it unaided to the upper floor of the house. Later, however, when she came out of her solitude, her penances and the flame that burned within her had reduced her weight and her strength by half.

---

[1] St. Euphrosyne is said to have cut her hair short and dressed like a man so that she could enter a monastery in Alexandria.—Tr.

No doubt these are details which Raymond learned from her mother, Lapa, who outlived her by many years. In accordance with the prevailing custom, the family began to think about getting Catherine a husband, but she scarcely gave the matter a thought herself and literally used to disappear whenever she saw a young man approaching. Lapa enlisted the help of Catherine's eldest and favorite sister, who was more successful, showing her how to make the most of her looks and, in particular, how to tint her beautiful hair. However, when this sister died in childbirth, Catherine was overcome with grief and regarded her sister's death as a punishment from God. She returned to her former resolve, but from then on she was never able to lament sufficiently her passing weakness.

The eldest sister's death only made the family all the more determined to have Catherine married. Not only was it to their interest to find her a husband but the marriage of a daughter was, naturally, the business of the whole family. Catherine, however, cut off her hair to show them how serious she was in rejecting their plans. When they saw what she had done, there was a scene, with Lapa crying aloud her disapproval and everyone vainly trying to compel Catherine to give up what they believed was merely a childish whim. When she would not give in, they deprived her of her freedom, made her do all the housework, and continually mocked, humiliated and reprimanded her. It was then that she discovered the necessity of building her cell within herself, a cell within her soul that she need never leave and in which she could remain alone with God. Then, too, she learned how to be with God throughout the day by seeing Christ, the Blessed Virgin, the Apostles and the disciples in the persons of those whom she had to serve with a smile.

In the end, her never-failing willingness and good humor won out, and at the propitious moment she revealed her secret: the vow that she had made as a child but the meaning and merit of which she now understood better than ever—to belong to Christ alone. This time her father took her part, giving her permission to lead at home the life she desired. Lapa now had to surrender but, understandably, she worried continually about her daughter's health when she saw her mortifications growing in severity.

Catherine had made up her mind to put her vow under the protection of St. Dominic by receiving the Dominican habit as a *Mantellata*.[2] These *Mantellate*, as they were called in Siena because of the black cloak they wore, were quite numerous there but they accepted only widows as members. However, they yielded to Catherine's insistence and, despite her youth, allowed her to join them, the first unmarried girl to do so.

In her *Dialogue*, when introducing the various founders of religious orders, she depicts God as describing St. Dominic and his ideals as follows:

"His task was that of the Word, My only-begotten Son. He was such an apostle in the world that, by spreading the truth and light of My Word, he was able to banish darkness. He was a light given to the world through Mary, in accordance with My will."

(*Dialogue*, Chap. 158.)

Catherine dictated this in her mature years, but what did she think of the matter when she was just entering the religious state "so spacious, so joyous, so perfumed," where one need think only of God's glory and the salvation of souls? When she took the habit, she was only eighteen. In what light did she then see herself as a member of the Dominican Order? What we do know for sure is that she shut herself in the small

2 The *Mantellate* were members of the Third Order of St. Dominic who lived in their own homes, led an austere life and wore a religious habit of black and white.—Tr.

room in her home that she had turned into a cell, never leaving it except to go to the Dominican church close by, never breaking her silence except to go to confession, and pushing austerity to its limits in abstaining from food and sleep. Above all, her cell became a tabernacle of the most extraordinary supernatural wonders, for visions, ecstasies and mystical graces of all kinds filled her days and nights:

She was able to find a desert in her own home and to make a solitude for herself in the midst of the world. . . . Catherine often said to me that it would be hard to find two people who had held such long conversations with one another as she had enjoyed with the Savior of men: "He spoke to me just as I am speaking to you."

(*Life*, Part 1, Chap. 9.)

Yet, she also experienced darkness and temptations, especially against her vow of virginity.

Toward the end of the third year of this retired, ecstatic life, a final grace was given her as the crowning of all the others when she was "espoused in faith" by Christ. What else remained after that? What was to be the climax of such a life? How could she become more withdrawn from the world, or reach greater heights?

However, one day Catherine, who ate nothing and who thought only of heaven, received an abrupt command from Christ: "Go, it is dinner time. . . . Go and join [your family]." The page on which Raymond relates this scene provides plenty of material for study, yet here we need only remark that this command was sufficient to send Catherine out into the world, first of all to the poor and the sick.

During these years of formation by the Holy Spirit, she was taught the basic principles that were henceforth to guide her life and actions:

7

"Daughter, do you know who you are and who I am? If you know these two things, you will be blessed. You are she who is not; I am He who is. . . . Daughter, think of Me; if you do so, I shall immediately think of you."

(*Life*, Part 1, Chap. 10.)

Faith in God's loving vigilance should free us completely from preoccupation with self, so that our actions express our love of God and our only goal in life is union with Him in order to please Him. Catherine learned what it was to have one's soul plunged in God, acting only with regard to Him and feeling nothing except through Him, as a diver in the sea lives and moves in it and feels and perceives everything through it. She came to know the necessity of "hating oneself" in order to root out self-seeking and self-love in all its forms.

She also learned the value of every suffering that makes the soul more like Christ, and her Master also imparted to her the secret of Christian strength:

"Therefore, daughter, for My sake, receive as bitter that which is sweet and as sweet that which is bitter; and then, have no doubt about it, you will be strong in every eventuality."

(*Life*, Part 1, Chap. 11.)

Espoused to Christ in faith, she became to Him "another self through a union of love." What a contrast between the plenitude of loving wisdom and the world which she discovered outside the walls of her cell!

In three incidents which Raymond relates one after the other, we see Catherine fighting evil; first, treating with smiling patience an ungrateful woman who was only angered by kindness; next, when she encountered another woman whose envy had turned into obstinate hatred, she repaid her by praying still more obstinately until she won mercy for the culprit; and when a sick widow whom she was nursing began spreading vicious calumnies about her out of malice and envy, she met the attack with simplicity, smiling silence and a redoubling of kindness and heroic service. In each of these victories over herself she experienced anew the love of Christ and was drawn even closer to Him.

Blessed Raymond, who heard of these events from the Saint herself, and all her other biographers after him, lay great stress on these incidents, for they were the peaks or climaxes of her first works of charity. Of course, these were not isolated events but rather presupposed and entailed an increasing involvement on Catherine's part with the world in which they took place: they were only three occasions among many others that were beginning to fill Catherine's life more and more, giving her a new form of the apostolate to accomplish. She was always ready to help when called upon, but she also came to realize that God was "reserving" the most difficult or painful cases for her.

Among the extraordinary graces that continued to make her union with Christ ever closer, the richest in symbolism was undoubtedly the exchange of hearts between our Lord and her. It happened like this. One day when she was begging Christ to give her "a clean heart," she felt that He took her heart from her body; then, a few days later, He returned and gave her His own heart instead. From that time on, she was conscious of loving God and her neighbor with Christ's own heart.

Another divine favor prepared her for her destined role in life. In the summer of 1370, if Raymond's dates are accurate, an extraordinary event occurred which was to enable her to feel as did St. Paul, whose name she "could not pronounce without great and visible joy." She came to know what it was to be "anathema . . . for the sake of [one's] brethren," to feel the contrast between the joys of possessing divine love

9

in its essential reality and the groaning misery of a world that could be saved only through suffering. At the time, she was only twenty-three and a half years of age, yet so far as she herself and those around her could judge, she appeared to die. Christ then seemed to reveal her fate to her, offering her a choice, either to go immediately with Him to heaven or to return to the world to work for her neighbor's salvation. We cannot gauge the objective reality of this vision, yet Catherine afterwards related it explicitly as she experienced it.

To put a seal on the close relationship of these three years and to demonstrate its definitive character, Christ espoused Catherine in the Faith while the citizens of Siena outside were busily engaged in celebrating their carnival. This mystical experience reiterated God's intention to wed her soul to Himself and repeated the Pauline phrase: "He who cleaves to the Lord is one spirit with him." When His divine bounty had begun to overcome Catherine, Christ had given her His heart as a pledge of His intention to express in her His own life.

The mysterious death that Catherine experienced some three years after her active life had begun engraved on her heart what St. Paul had himself felt: namely, the torment of an apostolic soul when the joy of being loved by God in Christ becomes a pain as vast as the joy. She, too, experienced this internal strain felt by the Apostle, for whom to live was Christ and to die was gain but whose presence in the world was needed for Christ's work.

Finally, five years later, on April 1, 1375, when Catherine's public mission was about to set her travelling the roads of the world, the fiery stigmata were given to her so that she could share in the sufferings of the Redemption. St. Paul himself had drawn reassurance from this thought: "Henceforth let no man give me trouble, for I bear the marks of the

Lord Jesus in my body" (Gal. 6:17). Apparently, by this gift of the stigmata, Christ completed the formation of the apostolic soul in Catherine, while her mystical experience had brought her preparation to a close.

Now she was drawn more and more to the Eucharist; her Communions plunged her into an ecstasy in which she passed from the Eucharist to the Trinity, as we can gather from her own words spoken at the time. The extraordinary graces that she experienced from then on seemed to be aimed especially at showing her the world's distress and the Saviour's merciful intentions in order to stimulate her desire and generosity in fulfilling her mission. But, in particular, she was given the message which she was to pass on to the world.

2. Personal Apostolate

LIKE all saints called to the active life, Catherine ministered to the poor and the sick—a form of charity which brought her into contact with wretchedness of soul and body; and when she met with envy, hatred and calumny, she overcame them with a smile. It is true that the virtues she practised are common in the lives of most saints, yet they are none the less admirable for all that.

Very soon, however, Catherine was to begin a mission altogether unusual among women saints: namely, that of making converts and acting as a spiritual director. Her role in making converts was apparently unique in the annals of the saints up to that time because hitherto women had not been called to take a direct part in the apostolate. It may be possible to find resemblances between her and some women missionaries in this respect, yet her "direct" action appears to be her exclusive privilege. Moreover, this apostolate of hers cannot be waved aside as a mere legend because in 1376 Pope Gregory XI issued a bull which provided that she was to be accompanied by three confessors with special faculties to absolve the sinners she converted. There are also letters which refer to her prodigious work in this respect, work which "crushed the devils" and "devoured souls." In particular, Fra Raymond describes the crowds of sinners that gathered around her as if summoned by "an invisible trumpet." He speaks of his long hours in the confessional, lasting from dawn to dusk and preventing him and his companions from eating anything "until the time for Vespers." With all simplicity, he describes his own weariness and Catherine's exuberant joy:

With my own eyes, I have at times seen a thousand persons and more, both men and women, flocking together as though summoned by an invisible trumpet and coming from the mountains or other parts of the country around Siena in order to see and hear the Saint. Not only her words but even the very sight of her was enough to make them repent of their offenses. They would weep, bemoaning their sins, and would crowd around the confessors. I was one of these confessors, and I found in these penitents such lively contrition that no one could doubt the great abundance of graces that had come down from heaven into their hearts. And that happened, not merely once or twice, but very often. The Sovereign Pontiff, Gregory XI, of happy memory, convinced and delighted by all the good that was thus being done in souls, for this purpose granted me and my two companions, by special apostolic letters, powers equal to those of the bishop of the diocese to absolve those who came to seek out Catherine and asked to go to confession. I call upon the Sovereign Truth Himself, who does not deceive and who is not deceived, to witness that we saw coming to us a number of great sinners, heavily burdened with vice, who had never before gone to confession or who had never received the sacrament of penance with proper dispositions. My companions and I frequently remained fasting until the time for Vespers without being able to hear all those who wanted to go to confession. To my own shame and to Catherine's glory, I must even admit that the crowd of penitents was so great that several times I felt worn out and irritated because of all the work involved. But Catherine never stopped praying and, like a conqueror who has just captured his prisoners, she overflowed with joy in the Lord, recommending her spiritual sons and daughters to look after us

13

who held in our hands the net she had cast for the haul. Pen cannot describe the plenitude of joy that filled the Saint's soul and the way she showed it exteriorly. And we rejoiced so much in her happiness that we forgot about our own weariness.

(*Life*, Part 2, Chap. 7.)

In some of these conversions Catherine intervened only by prayer. For example, a certain important citizen, notorious for his debauchery and crimes, remained obstinately impenitent and refused the ministrations of Catherine's confessor until she appeared to him as he lay dying and implored him to save his soul. Again, there were two condemned criminals who were not only obstinate, rebellious and impenitent but who added blasphemy to their other crimes. When, from her window, Catherine saw these men passing in the tumbril on their way to execution, she prayed for them and obtained for them the grace of repentance.

We know about the case of Nicola di Tuldo from the account which Catherine gives, without mentioning names, in one of her letters to Fra Raymond (Letter 273). Nicola was a young nobleman who had been unjustly sentenced to death for a political offense. Storming up and down his prison cell like a lion in a cage, he refused to receive the sacraments and turned savagely on the monks and priests who tried to approach him in his despair. Finally, Catherine herself came to see him, spoke simply to him about the meaning of life and death and of Christ's love, which the crimes of men could not thwart, with the result that he received communion and died bravely and joyfully, assisted by Catherine, and repeating the holy name of Jesus and hers. She was then permitted to behold the glory of Nicola's soul as it was received by Christ and she was allowed to savor the joy there is in heaven over one sinner who repents.

Often, however, the incidents in which Catherine figured were much less dramatic and pathetic. For example, a certain lax religious came to see this young girl about whom everyone was talking, some out of curiosity, some out of hostility and a wish to find fault with her. One problem perplexed him; but Catherine's simplicity opened his eyes.

The conversion of Nanni di Ser Vanni is especially interesting. Nanni, a well-known citizen of Siena, had his hands stained with the blood of several men and in addition had four living enemies whom, with full deliberation, he hated bitterly. But even though he was fully aware of his state of soul, he refused to repent. Still he came to see Catherine, although unwillingly and only because he had been "urged by the exhortations of a holy man, William of England . . . but without promising to follow any of the advice she might give him" (*Life*, Part 2, Chap. 7). Catherine had a gracious greeting for him "who feared her as the snake fears the charmer." She spoke to him about his reason for visiting her, but he only repeated his intention of remaining as he was, hatred and all. She then pointed out the danger he was in, "using in turn words that wounded and others that poured oil on the wounds. But he, like a deaf adder, closed the ears of his heart." Finally, out of politeness, he consented to forgive one of his enemies, but grace, having once entered by this chink in his armor, went on to conquer him completely. Overcome with sorrow, he called on God to pardon him; and Catherine, having thanked the Lord for his conversion, confided to him:

Beloved brother, at last God's mercy has made you see the danger you were in. I spoke to you, and you scorned my words; then I spoke to the Lord, who did not reject my prayer. Do penance for your sins, lest the time of trial come upon you unawares.

15

In other cases, the conversion of the sinner took time. For example, Catherine spent a whole winter under the same roof with an old man named Saracini, bearing with his sarcasm and being forced to listen to his rantings against religion. Once before when he had been gravely ill, he had gone to confession out of sheer fright; but now he laughed at his momentary lapse into virtue and proclaimed aloud his firm resolve never to be as spineless again. In the end, however, Catherine's supernatural charm did its work, the old man became less sure of himself and, one evening, went so far as to ask her what he should do to obtain God's mercy. Repeating the lesson of the Gospel, she showed him that he must begin by pardoning others—advice which he followed by being reconciled with his worst enemy, whereupon he experienced the happiness of God's forgiveness.

In those times of enmities, revolutions and warring factions, a large part of the Saint's endeavors was devoted to making peace; but, ironically enough, the authorities in the republic of Siena became alarmed at her activities, which were in fact aimed only at healing some of their political divisions, but which in their eyes made her an ally of their hereditary enemies. We can guess how decisively she reacted when her patriotism was thus questioned and her apostolic work threatened.

Catherine possessed a miraculous gift of insight which often enabled her to see the state of soul of those with whom she spoke. Her words, therefore, went straight to the mark; and not only could she diagnose the ills that afflicted a soul but could also prescribe the remedy. Her growing activity in this respect was nourished on prayer and sacrifice and founded on the saving love of God, whose work she was doing and whose will she desired to follow in all things. For her, there could be no other reason for living on earth than working

16

for the salvation of souls. We can glimpse her motives and experiences in the advice she gave to Blessed Raymond:

With this end in view, take pleasure in being with the publicans and sinners; as for the others, love them greatly and be seldom with them.

(Letter 104.)

Less unusual in the story of the saints, although more surprising to our modern minds, is Catherine's role as a mother.[1] To a large group of people, composed of men and women, young and old, noblemen and paupers, clerics and lay people, religious of all kinds, and her own *Mantellate* sisters from Siena and Tuscany—to all of these, Catherine, a dyer's daughter, a member of the lower classes, who was to die when only thirty-three years old—to all of these she was *la dolce mamma*, their dear, gentle mother. Her spiritual director, Raymond, whom the Dominican Order had appointed as superior of the group of tertiaries gathered around Catherine, was no exception, for he regarded himself as both the "father and son" of *la dolce mamma*.

A score of people of many different types accompanied her to Avignon, on the occasion of her visit to the Carthusian monastery on the island of Gorgona. When she went to Rome, sixteen men and eight women took up residence with her, but it is said that a much larger number had wanted to follow her. Her own mother, Monna Lapa, was one of Catherine's "children," and because hospitality was a favorite virtue of "the family" and *la mamma*, their guests at their frugal meal often numbered thirty and sometimes forty. To supply the needs of the group they resorted to begging, one or the other of them being assigned to the task when Catherine herself

[1] In fact, we can quote other instances from the Middle Ages where a holy woman played a similar role, e.g., Blessed Angela of Foligno.

17

did not undertake it. We learn these details from an account of a miraculous "multiplication of the loaves." But while the chronicler recorded the miraculous incident, apparently he did not even dream of describing the humble daily routine, which would be of no less interest to us. As we would expect in the circumstances, Catherine's spiritual activities were greatly increased, for, while no legal or canonical ties bound the "family" together, some who had joined it for a short time only, remained united with it in spirit long after their departure.

However, when we speak of Catherine's "family," we are thinking especially of those who shared in her life to a greater or lesser degree and who very often accompanied her on her journeys. One thing that strikes us about these members of her "family" is their great diversity. They differed in age and sex; some were converted sinners who began to follow her immediately after reaching the decision that changed their lives completely; others had already attained a high degree of spirituality and were attracted by the joy of being able to speak with kindred souls about God's secret ways with men; some were uncultured, while others, on the contrary, were highly educated in secular and religious matters. For example, Blessed Raymond of Capua became Master General of the Dominicans, and Blessed Stefano Maconi was chosen Abbot General of the Carthusians, which indicates that Catherine's "family" was recruited from different schools of spirituality and that she guided each one accordingly. Thus on her deathbed she revealed to Stefano Maconi, one of the best loved of her spiritual sons, that his vocation was to the Carthusian way of life. Several members of the "family" were Catherine's sisters in the Dominican Third Order, the *Mantellate*, so named, as we have already said, because of their black cloaks and their habit of Dominican black and white; but others

18

were still bound by the ties of matrimony. Catherine's own mother, the fiery Monna Lapa, became a tertiary and joined the "family" to be closer to her extraordinary daughter.

Yet in the light of history and the events of past ages, we today may perhaps be most struck by the close bond that was forged between people belonging to opposing parties and to families separated by unforgivable offenses, hereditary hatred and even murders. The political factions were at daggers drawn, and, as we have seen, Catherine belonged to the *popolo minuto,* both by birth and by association, for some of her relatives and close friends were active in Sienese politics. But all these barriers disappeared within that "family" that knew no frontiers and exercised no regimentation, yet whose members had nothing in common with each other except that, for each and all of them, Catherine, although little more than a girl, was their *dolce mamma.*

The fact that Raymond of Capua and Stefano Maconi have been beatified allows us to assess the spiritual level of the "family," although it would be wrong to imagine that all the members were perfect. They, too, had their troubles and difficulties, which are perhaps more instructive than their victories, especially for us whose mediocrity condemns us to living with the failures or meager gains of our everyday life. Some members, like Francesco Malavolti, were constantly overcome by their evil tendencies, while others did not feel up to things and complained aloud. Such disturbances occurred frequently, and apparently Catherine was never aware of the difference her presence or absence made in these matters. There were even some grave problems, as, for instance, when a religious went so far as to reprimand and abuse Catherine and finally made off with the family funds.

But we must not exaggerate these elements of discord, for the spirit that prevailed around Catherine was openly fraternal. We are told of her endearing traits of simplicity and almost playfulness in her way of welcoming people and in admonishing and consoling them. Yet she also proclaimed the demands of divine love and no one was more vehement than she in denouncing the crimes of men, especially of those whom Christ had charged to be most faithful because they were His representatives. It would be completely false to imagine that this was the tone in which she spoke to her followers, the *caterinati*, as they were called. Instead, from the accounts and allusions that have come down to us, we receive the impression that unconcealed joy and fraternal simplicity reigned among them. Each one knew that he was loved and understood as an individual; he knew that he was continually under the eyes of one whose powers of insight were often miraculous but who loved him incomparably. Ordinarily, the first thing Catherine did was to take upon herself in God's sight the sins of her spiritual children; and after that, how could her reproaches hurt or anger anyone?

Furthermore, it was impossible to mistake the nature of her love, which was totally without self-interest and whose sole aim was to draw others to Christ. Writing to her most devoted disciple, she could say:

Strip yourself of every creature, of me first of all, and clothe yourself in the love of God and of all creatures for the sake of God.
(Letter 102, to Raymond of Capua.)

But she could also write: "Your soul . . . has become nourishment for me" (Letter 273, to Raymond of Capua)—a food which she took at the table of the Lord's sacrificial love. In the same spirit she wrote to Monna Mellina: "I do not want you to love me or anybody whatsoever, if your affection is not founded on God" (Letter 144).

This maternal love could be as demanding as it was tender, as frank as it was respectful of others. Catherine was not just being conventionally pious when she wrote:

Bear patiently with my defects and my words. If anyone points out your defects to you, be glad and thank the divine Goodness for having given you someone who looks after you and who attends to your interests in His presence.

(Letter 344, to Raymond of Capua.)

One of the concluding sentences in her letter of farewell to Raymond reveals the depth and disinterestedness of her love as well as the common ideal that bound them together:

Do not be grieved because you are far away from me. It would truly be a great consolation for me to have you near me, but I feel a much greater consolation and joy when I see the harvest you are reaping for Holy Church. And now I beg you to work at that harvest with redoubled zeal because it was never needed so much as now.

(Letter 373.)

One of the things that drew people to Catherine was the beautiful doctrine she never tired of teaching. Her greatest relaxation was to speak of God to souls capable of sharing her thoughts; and when she had a chance to do so, her strength and gaiety were visibly renewed. But if, on the contrary, she was not able to share with others the overflowing of her heart, she seemed feeble and almost lifeless. Her speech especially was an outpouring of the love, wonder and confidence that filled her heart: "My soul is possessed with such joy, such jubilation, that I am amazed it can remain in my body." Not only did her words influence those who heard them, but her whole being also radiated a mysterious power that led others

21

to virtue and "made them delight in God," for when they were near her they felt something of the divine beauty and goodness.

She was not content with beautiful words but knew exactly what to say to each person for his instruction. In the *Dialogue*, she repeatedly refers to the duty of fraternal correction, a form of love which urges us to admonish our neighbors so that they may become better Christians:

> "Sow virtue charitably and kindly, combining gentleness with severity. . . . What you ought to do is be compassionate. Judgment belongs to no one but Me [i.e., Christ]. . . . If you think you see sin in anyone, accuse yourself of it along with him, and always give proof of true humility."

> (*Dialogue*, Chap. 102, 105.)

This is what she herself did, and no one could feel hurt when she accused herself of the same sin as he and took it upon herself before God. How, then, could a sinner fail to be caught up in the surge of love and contrition that poured from her heart?

Even more, one of the most attractive traits of her personality and one of the most reassuring for her children was her absolute simplicity and straightforwardness, the fruit of a love for which every word was a service rendered and which expressed its thoughts fully, keeping nothing back.

One of the great regrets of her adult life is related by Raymond. She had scarcely emerged from a long ecstasy when two friars asked her, by the way, if she would accompany them on a visit they were going to pay to a neighboring hermit. Spontaneously she said "Yes," but without really intending or having the strength to go with them. As a consequence of having uttered this one unthinking word, she spent three days in tears (see *Life*, Part 2, Chap. 6). This transparent sincerity of hers, knowing nothing of subterfuge or polite prevarication, lends a special beauty to her letters.

A cry from her heart which echoes throughout the *Dialogue* and which, therefore, was recorded by her secretaries, shows us how great was her love for her spiritual children and how close were the bonds that held her to them:

I also ask it of You very specially for those whom You have given me to love particularly and whom You have made one with me. They will be my consolation for the glory and praise of Your Name if I see them started along this sweet, straight path, pure and dead to their own will and counsel, not judging others, or being scandalized and murmuring against their neighbor. O most sweet Love, I beg that none of them be snatched from my hands by the infernal demon, so that on the last day they may reach the final end, which is You, O Eternal Father.

(*Dialogue*, Chap. 108.)

Hence we, too, must reach the same conclusion as Raymond and can understand why he saw in Catherine's maternal love a reflection of Mary's:

That is why the Spirit of God inspired us all to call Catherine our mother, which was not an empty title because, in all truth, she was our mother. She carried us in the womb of her soul, not without groaning and pains, until she had formed Christ in us, and continually distributed to us the bread of sound and useful doctrine.

(*Life*, Part 2, Chap. 11.)

To a great extent, Catherine's correspondence was the extension of her personal apostolate, and in her burning words we can see her love for souls urging her to give them not only the Gospel but also her very heart.

3. Church Affairs

CATHERINE'S activities took on new dimensions in 1374 and 1375, when she began to take part in the public affairs of the Church, a development which is not surprising since it was merely an extension of her love of God and her neighbor. Many of her converts and friends were important figures in the civic life of Siena, Pisa and Florence, and through them her influence spread from private to political life. Even her merely occasional contacts with prominent men often had repercussions on public affairs. Thus when writing to Charles V about supporting the Crusade, she asked him to do three things: first, to strive for sanctity by remembering that he wielded his royal power on Christ's behalf; second, to be very solicitous about the way justice was administered in his kingdom, especially in regard to the poor; and third, to renounce war, for the love of Christ, forgive injuries and restore peace. This was true Christian diplomacy, intent only on spreading the kingdom of God in souls.

Catherine carried the whole Church in her heart, and everything that affected the Church was of importance to her. Her beautiful words of love of the Church and the duty of working for it were spoken during this period of her life, and from them we can clearly see the profound communion that was so mysteriously established between Catherine, who called herself in each of her letters "the servant and slave of the servants of Jesus Christ," and the Pope, who, because of his universal office, was "the servant of the servants of God." Furthermore, in the Middle Ages, anyone with a widespread reputation for sanctity was regarded as a sort of official personage whose support was sought because of his or her prestige with the people and because temporal and spiritual interests were inextricably bound together in public affairs. That is why, in order to win Siena over to his side, one of the harshest tyrants of the era told his envoys to interest the daughter of the Sienese dyer in his cause, no doubt by impressing on her the scandalous misdeeds of certain prelates which, in his eyes, justified his rebellion and gave it a semblance of legitimacy. But Catherine's answer to this opportunist was such as to leave no doubts about her opinion of his imagined "rights" (see Letter 28, to Bernabò Visconti).

In 1374 Catherine was twenty-seven years old, she had been a tertiary for ten years, and her fame had spread far beyond Siena. As a result, the Dominican General Chapter held in Florence in that year summoned her to appear before it to be examined as to her orthodoxy and spirit. But her obvious sanctity, deep knowledge of the mysteries of the Faith and profound appreciation of the meaning of the Church quieted all fears, so much so that the Chapter decided to give her spiritual "family" an official Dominican superior. Their choice for this office was a talented priest, experienced in the spiritual life and renowned for prudence, whose name was Fra Raimondo delle Vigne, but whom we know as Blessed Raymond of Capua.

When Catherine, accompanied most likely by Raymond, returned to Siena at the beginning of the summer of 1374, the

Black Death was raging there. During the fearful days which followed, as the epidemic ravaged the city taking a heavy toll of Catherine's relatives and friends, she and Raymond were brought close together by the sorrows and heroic self-sacrifice they shared. Not only that, but when he caught the plague while ministering to the sick, she cured him and worked many other miracles before his very eyes.

Raymond's presence beside her gave her solid support in her teaching and, among other things, she was indebted to him for a clear understanding of the spirit that guided her in her attraction to daily communion. In addition, she found in him a teacher with whom she could speak from the heart about the divine mysteries and the ideal of sanctity preached by the Gospel. At the same time, he brought her into close contact with the work of the Dominican Order and with the world-wide concerns of Christianity, thus teaching her how really to serve the Church.

From this period on, four specific matters engaged her energies of soul and body—the Crusade; the reform of the Church, particularly of the clergy; the need for the return of the Pope to Rome; and the end of the war between the Pope and the city of Florence[1]—objectives which were in-

[1] Before we take up each of these projects in turn, a brief historical survey of the period will not be out of place. In 1375 Florence began a war to the death against the Papacy and succeeded in enlisting the support of many of the other Italian republics. In March of that year, Gregory XI placed an interdict on Florence for its heinous crimes and its obstinacy in revolt, and was preparing to send an army of pitiless mercenaries against the city. The Florentines then appealed to Catherine with apparent sincerity but in reality only to gain time, with the result that she went to Avignon to plead their cause. She arrived there on June 18, 1376; the Pope saw her often, and on September 13 he finally left Avignon for Rome. A short time later she herself left Avignon for Siena. However, when Gregory experienced the difficulties confronting him in Rome, he made no secret of his dissatisfaction with Raymond and Catherine. Nevertheless, taking heart once more, he decided to send her to Florence as his ambassador for peace. But while the negotiations were going on, he died suddenly, leaving it to his successor, Urban VI, to sign the peace with Florence. Urban, although he had been elected at a conclave intimidated by the threats of the Roman populace, sincerely intended to reform the

dissolubly linked together. Thus, the Florentines' revolt and their implacable war against the Papacy created enormous difficulties and threw into high relief the urgent need for reform. However, if we are to pursue our study of Catherine's apostolic character, we must take up each one of these subjects in turn.

In common with Christendom at large and the Papacy in particular, Catherine ardently desired to see the beginning of the Crusade for which the Pope was preparing. In July of 1375, Gregory XI appointed Raymond as one of the three commissaries selected to preach the Crusade and to collect the written pledges of those who had decided to take part in it. But what did the Crusade mean to Catherine? This is not the place to recall the question of the Crusades and the differences of modern opinion about them. And it would be unjust to judge the past on the basis of modern customs, ideas and conditions. Here we are interested solely in Catherine's motives for taking such an active interest in the Crusade. Raymond, who knew her equally well as a fellow worker and as a confidant, noted her three principal ideas. But we must remember that, when he spoke of the matter, several years had passed since the Saint's death; and we must not forget that, because of the schism, which continued to grow more bitter, the idea of a Crusade and indeed of Christianity as a whole was daily growing weaker. In addition, the Crusade was greatly hindered by the fact that Catherine's prophecies about it did not come true. She spoke of "the mystery of the holy passage" as an essential part of it; she dreamed of be-

---

Church. But since he was a violent and even brutal man, who nonetheless was easily offended, the Cardinals decided to elect another Pope, thereby starting the so-called "great Western Schism." We say "so-called" because everyone concerned sincerely believed that only the successor of St. Peter had authority to rule the Church. Yet for thirty-nine years they were split into opposing camps while they sought to determine who exactly was St. Peter's successor, the one to whom they could give their undivided loyalty.

coming a martyr in it, "of shedding her own blood for love of Christ's Blood." The benefits she expected from the Crusade, apart from the more immediate ones of defense against the Moslem invaders and the liberation of the Holy Sepulchre, were "peace in Christendom, penance done by those who wage war, and the conversion of many Saracens." These, Raymond insists, were the motives that most inspired Catherine to go to Avignon. In her letter to Charles V, she plainly states her reasons for urging him to partake in the Crusade; and her words are all the more striking when we realize that she considered unlawful the war Charles was waging to win back his lands from the English, a re-conquest which sixty years later was to bring Joan of Arc to her death:

Do you never think of the evils you are causing by not doing what is in your power to do? Evils for Christians and evils for the infidels, since your quarrels have prevented and are still preventing the fulfillment of the mystery of the holy passage. This misfortune alone, I believe, ought to make us fear God's judgment. I beg you not to cause so much evil any longer and not to hinder such great benefits as the deliverance of the Holy Land and of those poor souls who do not share in the Blood of the Son of God. You ought to blush for shame, you and all the other Christian princes. It is a great disgrace before men and an abomination before God that brother wars against brother while the enemy is left in peace, that we should wish to seize what does not belong to us and abandon what is ours by right. Enough of this folly, enough of this blindness! I say to you on behalf of Christ crucified—do not delay in making this peace. Make peace and turn your weapons against the infidels. Help to support and raise up the standard of the holy Cross.

(Letter 235.)

But something else troubled Catherine even more than the wars between Christian peoples, and that was the scourge of the times—the "great companies" or *condottieri*, those mercenaries who offered their services to the highest bidder among the belligerents and who, when peace was restored, lived off the countryside by pillaging or by holding the inhabitants up to ransom. She witnessed the fear of the citizens of Pisa when they were threatened by one of these bands of mercenaries, but fortunately she was able to intervene and save the city. With Raymond as her intermediary, she made the formidable captains promise to go on the Crusade; for if they were not only willing to make war but even regarded it as a kind of sport, why should they not turn their "sport" to a useful purpose by fighting against the common enemy? Catherine was also thinking of the mercenaries' souls, for she was deeply convinced that every service rendered to the Church, even though it was only material and performed from imperfect motives, was of value in God's sight. In expressing this conviction, she wished to bring out clearly the value of service to God done well and with a pure intention.

Finally, she was thinking of the salvation of many infidels; but it is hard to see the connection between the Crusade, which was a military expedition, and the conversion of the Saracens. Was this conversion to be effected by establishing the Church in the way intended by the Frankish kingdom of Jerusalem? It is certain that, without alluding to the missionary activity of her day, Catherine prayed "for the salvation of the whole world," which was one of the problems that was to inspire her *Dialogue*. She speaks of world conversion in a letter to Raymond in which she sets down beforehand the theme of her book:

"Know, daughter, that no one can escape My hand. Open the eye of your mind and see My hand." She looked and saw the whole universe enfolded in God's hand.[1] And God said: "I wish

1 We are reminded here of Christ's reference to His Father's hand in John 10:29.

you to know that no one can escape Me. Everyone depends on Me, either on My justice or My mercy. All belong to Me because they came from Me. I love them with an ineffable love and I shall show mercy to them by means of My servants."

Besides the Crusade, the idea of Church reform was very much alive at this period of history because the ravages of the Black Death and all the evils that followed it had shaken the world, particularly the spiritual world. Catherine longed for reform with all her heart and in words of poignant sorrow and breathless desire asked it of God and the Pope. She wanted it out of love for Christ crucified, so that the Blood of the Redemption might achieve its full efficacy, and for the glory of God in the salvation of souls. She had understood the urgency of reform from the time she had gone out into the world, where she had seen the gulf between humanity as it was and the divine ideal. But, thanks to her sound concept of the Church and to Raymond's influence, she did not go astray as did many contemporary "Spirituals" and later reformers with their apocalyptic visions and their disruptive ideas of the Church and its divine institution. On the contrary, she understood with her whole soul that reform was a growth of charity and a renewal of vigor in the universal Church; and she saw that if the reform was to achieve Christ's aims, it had to be carried out by the Church itself. That is why she never ceased asking God for it in prayer and begging the Popes, first Gregory XI and then Urban VI, to bring it about. The evil results of the schism that divided the Church did not cause her to lose sight of this essential ideal. She dared to point out even to the fearsome Urban VI that external preoccupations, especially his struggle with the antipope and the war that resulted from the schism, should not turn his attention away from undertaking a reform, and that he should begin with himself:

Most Holy Father, this is the sword I beg you to brandish. It is time to unsheath it and to detest sin in yourself, in your subjects and in the ministers of Holy Church. I say "in yourself" because no one today can say that he is guiltless of all sin; and each of us should begin by looking to his own soul.

(Letter 305.)

It was no part of Catherine's thought or mission to advocate institutional means of reform such as were employed two or three centuries later; for example, the erection of seminaries, the re-establishment of community life, and the multiplication of retreat centers. With a keenness of vision derived from supernatural enlightenment, she saw the evils among the clergy around her, which, sad to say, history records—the traffic in benefices, the predominance of material considerations, priests without vocation and without zeal. She visualized reform coming from above downward, with the Pope choosing cardinals who were fitted to become "pillars of the Church" and who, in turn, would gather about them fellow workers worthy of their mission. She stressed the duty of fearlessly reprimanding the sins and negligences of those responsible and the need for a general effort to combat the laxity of the clergy. She pointed out the necessity of promoting true priestly virtues among the clergy, especially zeal for souls and an unsparing vigilance for their salvation, or, as we would say nowadays, an ardent apostolic zeal springing from the love of Christ and an awareness of the immense responsibility involved in dispensing the fruits of the Redemption.

Catherine's conception of the necessary reform was a very simple one: it should be a return to that state of the early Church "when her ministers thought only of God's glory and the salvation of souls, applying themselves to spiritual things and not to temporal affairs" (Letter 206, to Gregory XI).

This does not mean, however, that she was an apostle of narrow rigorism or unmitigated severity. Very much to the contrary, she stressed the fact that the greatest sinners were least able to bear punishment:

God wills you to work at the reform of Holy Church, the punishment of abuses, the appointment of virtuous pastors. . . . In every case punishment should be meted out to the guilty party, yet not in the proportion he deserves, because the more he deserves it the less he can bear it, but rather to the extent that he is able to support it.

(Letter 267, to Raymond of Capua.)

She also emphasized to the Pope the need for reform:

The world is in such a state of upheaval, how shall peace be restored to it? . . . First you must pluck out of the garden of Holy Church those flowers that spread the infection of impurity, avarice and pride: that is to say, the bad pastors and superiors who poison and corrupt this garden. O you who are our master, use your power to pluck up these flowers. Cast them away so that they shall have nothing more to govern and so that they may concentrate on ruling themselves by living a good and holy life. In this garden plant sweet-smelling flowers: that is, pastors and superiors who are true servants of Jesus Christ and fathers of the poor, who seek only the glory of God and the salvation of souls.

(Letter 206, to Gregory XI.)

This concept of Church reform increasingly became both a torment and a hope to Catherine and in her eyes was identified with the idea of priestly holiness. As we have said, that was always her thought, but the more the terrible scourge of "clerical sin" threatened, the more clearly she understood the need for reform. As early as the end of June 1378, when she felt the danger near, she wrote to Urban VI:

Sweetest Father, the world cannot bear any more of this—so much do vices abound, especially in those who should be like sweet-smelling flowers in the garden of the Church. . . . We see them give themselves over to vices so shameful and so blameworthy that they infect the whole world! Renew completely the garden of your Spouse; put in it good and virtuous plants; surround yourself with a brigade of saints . . . who do not fear death. Do not stop at the very beginning. . . . Create a college of good cardinals as steadfast as pillars.

(Letter 291.)

In a later chapter we shall study the concept Catherine had formed of priestly vocation and sanctity. From the time of her arrival in Rome on November 28, 1378, which was some weeks after she had finished dictating her *Dialogue,* she strove to make the Pope share her opinion and decide to gather together in Rome a college of saints, ascetics and mystics who would be able to assist the Papacy with their prayers and advice. On December 13, just over two weeks after her arrival, the Pope signed a bull endorsing her plan, and she set about using every resource at her command to put it into effect, sending letters far and wide to persuade her closest friends and those most famed for sanctity to come to help her in Rome. But among her cruellest disappointments were the refusals she received from some of those to whom she had appealed but who preferred their solitude to serving the Church as she asked. However, others did answer her call by coming to form around her in Rome the community or family which we have already mentioned.

A prayer which Catherine uttered in ecstasy on the following February 20 shows us her conception of the role of prayer before God:

O most sweet Love, You have also seen in Yourself the needs of Holy Church and the assistance it requires. You have given it that assistance

33

in the prayers of Your servants whom You wish to raise as a buttress to support the wall of Holy Church. That is why the clemency of Your Holy Spirit inspires Your servants with such ardent desires for reform.

(Prayer 7.)

The war between Florence and the Pope was a terrible reality in which the Florentines used every means available, political, military and subversive, to gain the victory. Yet the grave and, at times, scandalous wrongs committed by certain legates or administrators of the Holy See, in violent contrast to the divine authority confided to Peter and his successors, made the war an atrocity in which good and evil were inextricably mixed.

Catherine did all she could to intervene with the Pope on behalf of those who were to blame, begging him for mercy and for peace. She also did her best to persuade the Florentines to submit, do penance and become once more the faithful children of their Father in the Faith. Catherine's official role, its nature and scope, are open to discussion and some doubt can be cast on it because it is not mentioned in the Papal archives, although there are contemporary witnesses whom, however, we may suspect of partiality or exaggeration. Yet we know that she had the soul of a mediator, taking upon herself the crimes of others and thinking only of peace. In fact, Gregory XI was so impressed with her that, at the end of her first audience with him during which Raymond acted as interpreter, he said to her, as Raymond relates:

So that you will see clearly that I desire peace, I put it entirely in your hands. Be solicitous only for the honor of the Church which I confide to you.

(*Life*, Part 3, Chap. 6.)

During all of this apostolate, which absorbed Catherine's attention for a long period of time and the need for which was the great sorrow of her life until the schism began, three main thoughts were uppermost in her mind: the love of peace, disinterestedness in temporal matters, and the spirit of faith in regard to the Church and its ministers.

For her, war and hatred were radically opposed to the intentions of Christ crucified, who had come to bring peace and overcome war and hate. Thus we find her using the expression "war against war and hatred." She continually begged for peace and kept on repeating that peace and not war would triumph over Florence, for peace was the weapon of the Lamb of God, whose Vicar was the Pope: "With peace you will overcome war and the hatred that divides souls, whom you will then re-unite once more" (Letter 209, to Gregory XI).

She often came back to the Pope's duty to rise above personal offenses, unjust calumnies and the depredations of the republics and to keep his eyes fixed solely on the salvation of souls and the glory of God.

Finally, she always felt keenly, and fervently wished to atone for, the violent persecution of the Church that was being conducted under the pretext of correcting abuses. As she saw it, striking at the Church was striking at God Himself. Continually she repeated to the Florentines:

You are well aware that Christ has left us His Vicar and that He has left him to us for the salvation of our souls, because otherwise we cannot have health, which is found only in the Mystical Body of Holy Church, of which Christ is the Head and we the members. And he who will not obey this "Christ on earth," who represents Christ in heaven, will not share in the benefits of the Blood of the Son of God. For God has willed us to receive this Blood from his hands, as well as all the sacraments of Holy Church, which give us life through this Blood. . . . You see, therefore, my well-beloved children, that anyone who rebels against Holy Church and our Father falls into death like a rotten member, because whatever we do to the "Christ on earth," we do also to Christ in heaven, who is the object of both our homage and our offences.

(Letter 207, to the nobles of Florence.)

In her role as peacemaker, Catherine hoped for only one thing for herself: the privilege of cementing with her blood one stone in the edifice of the Church.

As regards the Pope's return to Rome, the whole matter was a very complex one. Ten years previously, Urban V, whom the Church later beatified for his heroic virtues, had attempted to return permanently to Rome. However, in the face of agitation by the Romans, he had gone back to die in Avignon with the purpose of thereby assuring the freedom of the conclave that would meet to elect his successor. Avignon had many disadvantages as a location for the Holy See, especially since Urban V's successor, Gregory XI, was over-inclined to favor his relatives by installing them in important positions. Yet Rome, too, had disadvantages which had perturbed some great saints, among them St. Bernard. However, even before Catherine's arrival in Avignon, Gregory XI had already decided to return to Rome, although he yielded to the temptation to defer action and put off his return indefinitely.

Catherine certainly tried with all her strength and sanctity to support the Pope in making this very difficult and strongly opposed decision; and she no less certainly influenced him to leave Avignon abruptly: "It is better to burst one's bonds than to untie them." Therefore she deserves our praise for performing this important task in the life of the Church. She saw in the Pope's return to Rome a remedy for the Florentine war, for the grave defects of papal government through inter-mediaries, and a beginning of the reform which she so ardently desired. Her own words best express what was in her heart:

Come! Come, and do not resist any longer the will of God who calls you. Your hungry sheep wait for you to come to take and keep the place of your predecessor and leader, the apostle St. Peter. Your office as Vicar of Christ obliges you to live in your proper place. Come, then, come! Do not delay any longer! Take courage and do not fear what may befall you, because God will be with you!

(Letter 197, to Gregory XI.)

37

4. The Gift of Self to the Church

❖❖❖❖❖❖❖❖❖

W HEN Florence was reconciled with the Pope and peace restored, Catherine went back to Siena in August of 1378. She was acutely aware of the difference between the reality and the ideal peace of which she had dreamed but she knew from three years' bitter experience that the terrible evils caused by the sins of laymen rebelling against the Church were but "milk and honey" when compared with the scourges that were going to descend upon the world as a result of "the sin of the clergy." United as she was with the Church through love of Christ, she was about to enter upon the most crucifying phase of her apostolic life.

It was at this point that she set about satisfying a desire which she had nourished for some time: the yearning to leave behind her a book summing up her experiences and giving the substance of what she had learned. Following her usual method, she had warned her secretaries to be ready to take down whatever she would dictate while in ecstasy (see *Life*, Part 3, Chap. 1). But this procedure does not completely exclude the possibility that parts of the book might already have been drafted, for in one of her letters she refers to the "book" she had left in Florence. Accordingly, in October of 1378, in Fra Santi's hermitage, some seven miles from Siena, she

38

gathered around her several of her secretaries, whose names we know. While she was still at the hermitage, she received the shocking news that on September 20 at Fondi, not far from Rome, the cardinals had capped their revolt against Urban VI by electing an antipope, Robert of Geneva, who took the name Clement VII. The most terrible of schisms had begun.

Before we follow Catherine to Rome, we must pause to consider the dictation of the *Dialogue*, for it is one of the most important events in her life. During the previous year she had thought continuously about the book and had dreamed of setting down in it all she had learned about apostolic holiness. In a letter written about this time, she confided to Raymond that in October of the previous year she had asked God the main questions she wished to have answered on the subject of apostolic sanctity. God had given her the essential answers and now she wished to commit them to writing, for they summed up not only her mystical experiences but also her apostolic efforts. Perhaps it was thus that she had formed the idea of founding a race of souls who would love God to the extent of losing everything for His sake. In fact, this was what God had asked of her: "Daughter, conceive and give birth! Give birth to a race of men that shall hate sin and love Me with a great and burning love" (Letter 272, to Raymond of Capua).

A comparison between this letter and the *Dialogue* shows her general intention quite clearly. One of the requests she had made of God in October of 1377, concerned her "spiritual father," who had complained to her about his weakness although he knew that he was called to spend himself for the glory of God in the salvation of souls. Catherine prayed with all her heart for this intention and received in answer a clarification of Raymond's apostolic aspirations in the form of an instruction on the gift of Christ and ever closer union with Him in suffering and in spending oneself with Him. She wrote to Raymond as if in God's name:

"Therefore you should cross over this bridge, seeking the glory of My name in the salvation of souls, bearing many adversities bravely, and following the footsteps of the sweet Word of love. You are My workers whom I have sent to toil in the vineyard of Holy Church because I wish to show mercy to the world."

And a little further on:

"Up, My true servants! Learn of Me, the Word, to take the lost sheep upon your shoulders and bring them back at the cost of your sufferings, of many vigils and prayers. That is the way you will cross by Me, who am the bridge. You will be the children and the spouses of My truth."

(Letter 272, to Raymond of Capua.)

In the *Dialogue*, which is of general application and does not share in the confidential nature of a personal letter, this request is replaced by another which Catherine made on her own behalf. As a result, each reader can, as it were, identify himself with her as she receives the answer which is found in the section of the *Dialogue* usually called "A Treatise on Discretion." A better title would perhaps be "The Scale of Values," provided that we remember that, even here, the outlook is still apostolic:

Wishing to know and imitate the Truth more courageously, and sending up her plea first of all for herself (for she believed that one cannot truly help one's neighbor by teaching, example and prayer if one cannot first benefit oneself), this soul made four requests of the Supreme Father, the first being for herself. . . .

(*Dialogue*, Chap. 1.)

The soul has a twofold relationship—first to God the

40

Infinite and then to the neighbor; God, who is the Infinite Good, calls for infinite works which, however, will not be acknowledged as infinite except when performed in the effective service of the neighbor.

The other three questions were just as much on Catherine's mind. Her second request concerned the salvation of the whole world, or rather man's cooperation with God's intention to show mercy to the world. God's immense love has expressed itself in the gift of Christ to men as a bridge between heaven and earth, so that only those who are united to Christ will be saved, and only those who are united to Him to the point of being "other Christs" with Him in a union of love are His effective coworkers, spending themselves to unite their brethren with Him, the Savior of all. Here Catherine, in speaking about working "for the salvation of the whole world," repeated and developed the same ideas which she had already expressed when writing to Raymond about his apostolic aspirations. The fact that she did so throws into clear relief the nature of Christian sanctity, so completely orientated toward the glory of God in the salvation of souls. This is not to say that the *Dialogue* follows a rigid plan; it is, after all, a dialogue and, despite the profound unity of Him who reveals Himself in it, there are many digressions that cannot be fitted into a neat framework. It is even quite probable that the secretaries had an eye to underlining certain logical trains of thought, but their rather heavy hand has somewhat the effect of cement daubed clumsily over the tight joints of a dry-stone wall.

The third question and answer concerned the reform of Holy Church. The divine light revealed to Catherine the holy ideal conceived by God for His priests and the betrayals of which they were guilty. The contrast between the two was poignant indeed, but it did not lead Catherine to revolt or to a self-righteous withdrawal from the Church, as happened in the case of false reformers, but rather to an intensification of love, generosity and prayer. Neither inner catastrophes nor persecutions from outside were to renew the Church but solely an interior growth of faithful souls, for the Church is continually re-born of the one Spirit. We would misjudge Catherine if we concentrated on her anguish to the exclusion of the joy that filled her heart even in the midst of her sufferings, because she never lost sight of the fact that the Church is the bride of Christ, infinitely loved and always holy with the holiness of its Divine Spouse and therefore having no need of reform in itself. In addition, she was always aware that God prepares the remedy at the same time as men commit the fault.

In the fourth request, Catherine "begged divine Providence to provide for the needs of the world in general, and in particular for a certain matter that had arisen" (*Dialogue*, Chap. 1). The title "A Treatise on Divine Providence" is well chosen, for God does everything out of love, and human efforts must correspond and cooperate with this divine intention:

> "I have answered your fourth request. You wanted Me to provide for a certain matter, and, as you know, I have done so. It was in regard to this that I spoke to you about My Providence, in general and in particular, while showing you that, from the beginning of the world until the end, everything has been done and will be done by that Providence, because it is always I who send or permit whatever happens, trials or consolations, whether spiritual or temporal, in order to sanctify you and to accomplish My truth in you. There, in fact, is My truth: I created you in order to give you eternal life. This truth is shown to you in the Blood of My only Son."
>
> (*Dialogue*, Chap. 106.)

The whole book is organized around these four questions

which Catherine put to God in October of 1377. She could not write because she had never been taught, but she dipped deep into her memory and dictated what she had learned from God, especially in the fire of ecstasy, and what she had gleaned from her human contacts.[1] An appropriate title for her work would be *The Book of God's Teaching*, however, the usual title is the *Dialogue*, which has the advantage of informing the reader that he is not about to start on a course of didactic instruction but rather that he is going to take part in a conversation—one could almost say in a tragedy if it were not for the fact that, despite the critical circumstances of the times, the book hurries on to a merciful climax. In fact, the questions posed by the Saint seem merely incidental, while God's answers are the essentials.

Catherine, then, was engaged in dictating her *Dialogue* when she heard the news of the schism and received Urban VI's summons to come to Rome. The connection between the *Dialogue* and this urgent need on the Church's part does not arise simply from a coincidence of dates but springs from a much deeper source. When reading the book, we must remember that the sanctity which makes every disciple of Jesus "another Christ" is the best answer to the evils of one's times and the best service one can render to the Church. At the time, however, Catherine was not able to foresee the duration and vicissitudes of the upheaval in which, for more than thirty years, Christianity was to be compelled to ask who was its true head on earth. This terrible trial has been called a schism, but incorrectly so, as we have already pointed out, because everyone concerned was agreed on the basic principle

---

[1] In general, historians are agreed that Catherine's "miraculous" knowledge of writing is an exaggeration by Caffarini, especially since Raymond, who would have been the first to benefit by it, does not mention it at all—surely remarkable reticence in a man who was not inclined to be reserved when it came to recording the Saint's gifts and accomplishments!

43

of the unity of the Church, namely, obedience to Peter's successor. Yet this schism (we shall retain the term for the sake of convenience) rent the Church grievously because no one knew who was the lawful Pope. As we have seen, the cardinals had elected two men, one after the other, and, having crowned the first and acknowledged him as Pope, they then proceeded to declare the second one the sole legitimate successor of St. Peter. A crisis of this nature was bound to bring home forcibly to all men the importance of the unity desired by God for His Church, the mother of His children.

For the year and a half which remained to her on earth, Catherine identified herself with the Papacy, taking up her abode body and soul in Rome, living out the tragedy and finally dying of it.

For some six years now, she had loved to call the Pope "Christ on earth." It was only to be expected then that, in the painful situation caused by the schism, she should be united more closely than ever to the Chair of Peter. We have already seen her efforts to gather around the Pope a company of spiritually minded people to assist him with their advice and prayers. But it is useless to go back over all that.

These last months of Catherine's life are characterized by her obedience to the Pope, her desire to serve him and her readiness to undertake any task at his bidding. Her uncalculating generosity, which made her eager to do everything she could, was a form of that obedience to the Pope which she valued so highly. She expressed her views on this matter very forcefully to Raymond when he thought he would have to give up his mission, which he believed was now impossible because of the ambushes which the antipope's followers had reportedly prepared for him:

If you had been faithful, you would not have fallen into such serious

44

hesitation and you would not have doubted either God or me, but, like a faithful and promptly obedient son, you would have gone forward to do what you could. And if you were not able to walk upright, you would have gone forward on your hands and knees; if you were not able to travel as a religious, you would have gone as a pilgrim; and when you lacked money, you would have begged for alms. . . . Such faithful obedience would have borne more fruit before God and in man's hearts than any human precautions. . . . I wish that, without pausing, you had set out at once by whatever means you had available. . . . We are offered like dead men in the garden of Holy Church to the owner of the garden, who is "Christ on earth." Let us act, then, like dead men. A dead man neither sees nor hears nor feels. Try to kill yourself with the sword of hate and love; try to kill yourself so that you will no longer notice the injuries, outrages, and reproaches of the persecutors of Holy Church, and so that you will no longer see the impossibility of your task or the probable trials.

(Letter 344, to Raymond of Capua.)

On the other hand, she could not even understand, and was vehemently indignant at, the idea that anyone could fail to obey the Pope, thus treating him like any ordinary authority:

He refuses to come, alleging that whoever is bound by divine obedience should not obey a creature. I shall not speak of other creatures, but when it is a question of the Vicar of Christ, that pains me deeply . . . because divine obedience never frees us from that obedience.

(Letter 328, to Fra Antonio da Nizza.)

Despite the unrelenting efforts of Catherine and her followers, all seemed lost. She wrote to Raymond:

Day and night God compels me to concern myself with many other matters, all of which fail because of my sins, which are perpetual

45

hindrances to good. Alas, we are drowning in the mounting flood of iniquities, which shall be severely punished. I live in sorrow. May God's mercy snatch me quickly from this dark life!

(Letter 344.)

Immediately after his election, the antipope Clement VII had begun a war against Urban VI. But the fall of Castel Sant' Angelo after months of siege, and a military defeat at the hands of Urban's supporters, only resulted in Clement's installing himself in Avignon and the consolidation of the schism since France was solidly behind the antipope. But even worse, the new cardinals created by Urban fell into the same bad habits as their predecessors and thereby hindered the desired reform, while the Pope's own defects of character— his irritability, curtness, impulsiveness, violence and vindictiveness—jeopardized the most important undertakings and stultified the best intentions, so that even his friends and supporters were often offended and discouraged. Yet Catherine, like a watchful sentinel, continued to raise her voice and sound the alarm, for she was but the human echo of that Voice that spoke within her: "Tell My Vicar to do his utmost to be gentle and to give peace to those who want it. . . . Tell the pillars of the Church . . ." (Letter 371, to Raymond of Capua, according to Gigli).

However, the Saint's voice often went unheard, and matters reached such a pass that the people of Rome began to consider rising in rebellion and murdering Urban, whom they had come to hate. Everything seemed lost: not only did an antipope reign undisturbed in Avignon but the real Pope went in danger of his life in the heart of Rome! Catherine and her followers entered fully into the struggle, for she wished above all to calm the people. And He who desired to show mercy through His servants laid down His conditions:

46

During all of Lent, I was to offer to God all my followers' pleas and to have Masses celebrated exclusively for the intention of Holy Church. Such was the obedience that God laid on me.

(Letter 373, to Raymond of Capua.)

She prayed continually. Describing her daily life to Raymond, she wrote:

When the bells ring for Matins and I come out from Mass, you would see that I am like a real corpse as I go to St. Peter's. I enter there and set to work immediately in the barque of Holy Church. I stay there until evening and I should like not to have to leave that place day or night until at last I see the people to some degree steadfast and firm in their proper relationship with their Father.

(Ibid.)

During these desperate hours, she showed her love for Christ and the Church by her generous and unselfish devotion. Steadfastly she stayed at her post in the midst of this spiritual tempest where everything seemed lost were it not that Christ was there. Consumed as she was with love of Christ, she became a holocaust for the Church. Truly, in accordance with God's wish, "she was entirely consecrated in life, heart and love, solely to the spouse of Christ, without thought of self" (see Letter 371, to Raymond of Capua, according to Gigli). It was then that her mission took on its full meaning. Writing once more to Raymond, she said:

"O eternal God, receive the sacrifice of my life for the Mystical Body of Holy Church. I can give You only what You Yourself have given me. Take my heart and press it to the face of Your spouse." Then the eternal God, lowering the gaze of His clemency, took my heart from me and pressed it to Holy Church. He seized my heart with such violence that, if the help of His strength had

47

not immediately prevented the vessel of my body from breaking, life would have left me.

(Letter 371.)

Her heart squeezed of its last drop of blood to cleanse the face of the Church, the spouse of Christ, which is loved for His sake—this sums up the whole of Catherine's life. Her strangely beautiful expressions show clearly enough that we are not dealing with mere figures of speech but rather with symbols trying to translate the incommunicable personal relationship between God and the soul whom He loved and whom He made partaker of His own great love.

Catherine was now ready to die; she had given her whole being to God and her sacrifice was accepted. Her death itself was awe-inspiring and was, in the fullest sense of the word, the last act of her life, for it was her conscious and definitive return to Him who had sent her forth as His envoy. Here we need not have the least misgivings that the real facts may have been embroidered by Catherine's followers or by subsequent chroniclers. Everything recorded by those who witnessed her death is as true and as factual as the sanctity of her soul.

On the morning of April 29, 1380, she asked for the final absolution and received Extreme Unction. Then those who were gathered around her witnessed a struggle the full violence of which escaped them. Undoubtedly the devil was there in his terrifying role of accuser, for Catherine repeated some sixty times her humble prayer: "I have sinned, O Lord; have mercy on me!" After that she repeated other prayers. The struggle went on for about an hour and a half, and ended with Catherine's saying, "Not vainglory, but rather the true praise and glory of God!"

She had won the victory. Then, with one of her best loved disciples helping her to sit up and supporting her, she accused

48

herself before God of all the omissions of her life, comparing them with the greatness of the task assigned to her.[2] In the divine light of Him whom she had served, she saw plainly the gulf that still remained between her dream and the reality, but she knew that her shortcomings were forgiven. Once more she requested and received final absolution, with the indulgence promised her by Urban VI. She then went on praying for her disciples and spoke individually to some of them about various matters hitherto left unsettled, among them the vocation of her dear spiritual son, Stefano Maconi, who was to enter the Carthusians, where eventually he became Abbot General. She asked a blessing from her mother, who in turn begged her daughter to obtain for her from God the grace of not offending Him in her sorrow.

Then Catherine resumed her last prayer for the Church, for Urban VI, whom she declared once more to be the lawful Pope, and for her disciples. Finally, feeling that God was calling her to Him at last, she hastened eagerly to answer His summons, with the promptness of an obedient daughter, longing only for Him and depending upon Him alone. Aware of her own nothingness and her love for Him, she realized fully that all that she possessed she had received from Him:

> "Lord, You are calling me to come to You, and I am coming to You, not because of my merits but only because of Your mercy, which I ask of You in the name of the most sweet Blood of Your Son." Then she cried several times: "Blood, Blood!"
>
> (Barduccio Canigiani, in *Fioretti*, p. 187.)

And following the example of Christ, whose words she repeated once more, she commended her soul to God, bowed her head and breathed her last sigh.

---

[2] We shall give her own words in full when we speak about humility in a subsequent chapter.

5. Holy Desire

THE Blessed Virgin received Him who is the Gift of God and learned by that unique experience the preferences of the One who thus gave Himself, as she tells us in her *Magnificat*: "He has filled the hungry with good things." Later, as Catherine puts it, "The Lord said: 'Let him who thirsts come to Me and drink.' He does not invite anyone who is not thirsty" (Letter 318, to Sano di Maco and others).

It is important to stress how urgently Catherine's insistence on this point was needed as a remedy by the era of defeatism, sensuality, fear and egoism in which she had to proclaim her message. For the desires of God's servants must correspond with His wishes, and when He wills to show mercy to the world, His apostles must draw down this mercy and transmit it by their desires. That was a basic tenet of Catherine's teaching. As God said to her,

> "There is a remedy [for the ills of the world], and that remedy is My servants if they are zealous enough to constrain Me with their tears and to bind Me with the bond of their desire."
>
> (*Dialogue*, Chap. 15.)

At the most important period of her life, when God revealed to her that she and her disciples had a sacred duty to offer them-

selves for the Church, she could write: "Set yourself, therefore, never to slacken but rather always to increase your
desires" (Letter 371, to Raymond of Capua).

The desire of the one who prays and of him for whom one
prays opens the way to God's grace:

> "Suffering expiates only by virtue of the desire of the soul that
> unites itself to Me, who am the Infinite Good; and such a soul
> makes expiation to a greater or less degree according as the love
> of him who offers Me prayers and desire, and the love of him
> who is being prayed for, are more or less perfect. It is upon this
> offering which he makes to Me and to the one who is to profit
> by it that he will be judged by My goodness. Stir up, then, the
> fire of your desire, and do not allow a single moment of time
> to go by without the sound of your cries before Me and of your
> humble voice raised in incessant prayer for them."
>
> (*Dialogue*, Chap. 4.)

Catherine describes this desire in various ways: as an
unquenchable fire, as the torture of insatiable hunger or as a
thirst that cannot be satisfied; it is the torment that arises
from the lack of something that cannot be done without, or
the ardor of the lover for the object of his love. The human
heart, poor in its possessions yet infinite in its capacity, understands immediately the nature of desire. But why is desire
given such importance by Catherine?

When we speak of desire, we focus attention on the center
from which proceed all our interior and exterior acts: "It is
an undeniable fact that without this inner fire you will do
nothing either great or small" (Letter 344, to Raymond of
Capua). Thus our prayers, coming from our hearts and rising
to God on behalf of our neighbor, will be in turn a joy because of his goodness and a sorrow because of his sin and
wretchedness; and our prayers, drawn from Christ's heart,

will serve to refresh the members of His Mystical Body. That, in short, was Catherine's doctrine on prayer.

Desire makes us go out of ourselves, cuts the root of our self-complacency, and excludes the tendency to regard ourselves as the center of the universe or to make our likes and dislikes the standard for judging everything. We are not true apostles when we choose to do only what pleases us or when we act solely out of self-interest:

Open, open wide your soul to receive your neighbor by love and desire. Yet I cannot see how we can have this desire if our eyes are not turned, like the eyes of an eagle, toward the tree of life.

(Letter 70, to Fra Bartolomeo Dominici.)

This desire is fanned still more by our awareness of the world's distress, particularly when we compare this distress with the greatness of God. At the beginning of the *Dialogue*, Catherine says of herself:

Her desire was great and continual, but it increased much more when the First Truth showed her the need in which the world stood, and the storms and offenses against God in which it was plunged.

(*Dialogue*, Chap. 2.)

In this way the election of an antipope and the open war against the lawful successor of St. Peter were transmuted into desire.

In addition, since desire is a spiritual thing, it meets with God's demands, for He is a Spirit; and by becoming infinite through charity, it truly corresponds to what He wishes: it alone gives value to what we do and suffer for God: "I am infinite; I desire infinite love and infinite pain. . . ." All our sufferings, whether they are spiritual or temporal, and from whatever source they come, are finite works and are done in time, which itself is finite. But desire gives them an infinite value, so that they can make satisfaction for sins that deserve infinite punishment. The virtue of desire has acted in them, and hence they have infinite value.

When Catherine surveyed the failure of her own efforts and chided Raymond for what she considered his cowardice, she wrote: "I want nothing more; let us renew our lives and increase the flame of desire" (Letter 344, to Raymond of Capua). But desire does not deserve its name unless it is the expression of a dedicated soul: that was one of the first lessons which Catherine had learned from her Divine Master and which He recalled to her mind in the *Dialogue*. When she prayed that He would show mercy to the world, He replied by granting her an allegorical vision in which she saw a tree, without crown or root, representing God, who has neither beginning nor end. The foot of the tree rested on the earth, as in the Incarnation the divinity of the Word was united to the clay of our humanity. All around the tree grew a hedge of thorns, at the sight of which many people turned back and threw themselves on a pile of empty husks, deceptively attractive because they looked like full ears of grain. Many died of hunger as they grovelled among the husks, but others who were wiser returned to the tree and bravely pushed through the hedge of thorns to reach the shade and fruit it provided. The hedge that blocks the way to truth is the vacillation of the will, the continual struggle between conscience and sensuality, between the love of Christ and the love of self.

Once the soul has humbly but irrevocably declared that it wishes to follow Christ crucified, it is free to soar and finds unchanging goodness, peace, strength, joy and life. Then it can serve Him who wishes to show mercy to the world. At this point, *la dolce mamma* instructs it:

See that you are not lukewarm but burning to urge on your brothers and the leaders of the company. . . . By being what you should be, you will light up the whole of Italy, and that is not so difficult.

(Letter 368, to Stefano Maconi.)

This desire is, in the disciple, but a pale imitation of "that great love and that great desire" (Dante) that filled the soul of Christ. Catherine was fond of taking her inspiration from the divine words recorded by St. Luke: "I have greatly desired to eat this passover with you before I suffer" (see Letter 36). That is why "only those who have an infinite desire are united with Me by love" (*Dialogue*, Chap. 3).

For the rest, we must not forget that the Christian's desire is a sheer gift from Christ. The Christian begins to desire God's glory and the salvation of souls because, like Daniel, he is the object of God's desires, for God wishes to make him His collaborator by initiating him into the work of an apostle:

"You see that you have bound Me with this bond and that I Myself have given you this bond because I wished to show mercy to the world. If I give My servants this hunger and desire for My glory and the salvation of souls, it is because, constrained by their tears, I temper the wrath of My divine justice. Take your tears, then, and your sweat; do you and My other servants draw them from the fountain of My divine charity, and with these tears wash the face of My spouse because, I promise you, this is the means whereby her beauty will be restored to her. She will regain her beauty, not by the sword or by war or by cruelty, but by peace, humble and continual prayer, and the tears and sweat poured out with the anguished desire of My servants. . . . And I, too, say to you that I want you to act thus. Never lessen your desire to call on Me for help. Never lower your voice calling Me to show mercy to the world."

(*Dialogue*, Chap. 15, 107.)

Part 2: *Apostolic Sanctity*

❖❖❖❖❖❖❖

6. Redeeming Love

CATHERINE'S name and spiritual endeavors are indissolubly linked with the memory of Christ's redeeming blood. To express the connection between her words and the love of Christ, she began her letters: "I write to you in His Precious Blood." As we shall see more clearly in a moment, she believed that we "find fire in the Blood" of Christ, and that His Blood receives its efficacy only by virtue of His divinity (Letter 73, to Sister Costanza). Once, when she was praying for immaculate purity, she felt as if she were being sprinkled with a shower of blood and fire combined, an indication that such experiences are not so much imaginary phenomena as the expression of a spiritual mystery. She was profoundly impressed by the three elements that are really only one—water, blood and spirit; and if we are to understand her, we must clearly grasp the inner vision that inspired her actions.

If the apostolate were simply the highest form of human activity, we should have to enquire how it utilizes the different techniques of communication, especially the technique of the dialogue. In a dialogue on the apostolate, two free agents communicate with each other so that they may share the truth, so that they may exchange views on the most effective methods of ensuring the adherence of a free, intelligent being to God. But the apostolate is more than that: it is a cooperation in God's work, a collaboration in His designs and therefore a communion with His love acting in the world, re-adopting men by uniting them in the Mystical Body of His Son made man. Therefore, in order to understand an apostolic soul, nothing is more important than to discover its vision of the world and to know the viewpoint that enlightens and inspires its action, for that is the source from which external actions draw their strength and form.

This concept was dear to Catherine. We have already quoted her exhortation to one of her best-loved disciples:

Open, open wide your soul to receive your neighbor by love and desire. Yet I cannot see how we can have this desire if our eyes are not turned, like the eye of an eagle, toward the tree of life.

(Letter 70, to Fra Bartolomeo Dominici.)

The cross, the symbol of divine love, must have a fascination for the eyes of an apostle as, in the ancient legends, the sun drew to itself the gaze of the eagle.

Thanks to the notes made by Catherine's secretaries as she spoke, and to her letters and *Dialogue*, it is relatively easy for us to know what was in her heart and to become acquainted with the source from which sprang her gigantic apostolate; or, to be more exact, we can trace the ideas that inspired her life, for the inner workings of every soul are God's secret alone.

When Catherine prayed, she placed herself immediately in the presence of God, plunging at once into the mystery of the Trinity. For her, everything came from God—Father, Son and Holy Spirit—and to Him everything had to return. As proof of this we could quote the first words of any of her prayers; this one, for example, springing from the depths of her heart, expresses her attitude with particular force:

O eternal Trinity, O You who are madly in love [with mankind], what profit did You draw from our redemption? Truly none. What need had You of us, You who are our God? Who, then, profited by it? Man, and man alone! O incomprehensible charity!

(Prayer 17.)

It was in this light that Catherine perceived that man's dignity resulted from his relation with God and the divine image impressed on his soul. For her, the words of Genesis stating that God created man "to his own image and likeness" (Gen. 1:26) were a living light that stimulated her gratitude and increased her apostolic spirit:

O eternal Trinity and only Deity! O Deity, one Essence in Three Persons! You are a vine with three branches, if it is permissible for me to make this comparison. You have made man in Your image and likeness so that, by the three powers which he possesses in one soul, he may bear the seal of Your Trinity and Unity. Not only does he resemble You by these three faculties, but by them he is furthermore united to You. By his memory, he resembles and is united to the Father, to whom Power is attributed; by his intellect, he resembles and is united to the Son, to whom Wisdom is appropriated; by his will, he resembles and is united to the Holy Spirit, to whom clemency is attributed and who is the Love of the Father and Son.

(Prayer 23.)

But the Incarnation in particular fascinated Catherine because in it the mystery of God is best revealed to man. To do justice to her thought, we would have to quote all her words because her very human nature speaks to us of the humanity that God took in order to save us and unite us to Him. Yet she never stopped at Christ's humanity but, through it, entered the mystery of God's giving Himself to us and uniting us to Him:

61

So that my littleness might see Your greatness, You made Yourself
small, You enclosed the immensity of Your Divinity in the littleness
of our humanity, and You showed Yourself to us through Your Word,
Your only-begotten Son. In this way I have known You in myself,
O Abyss of Charity! Yes, it is thus, in the Word, O unfathomable
and eternal Trinity, O incomprehensible Love, that You have showed
Yourself, that You have revealed to us Your Truth, especially by the
outpouring of His Blood. . . . This Blood is a further testimony to
Your charity; it tells us that out of love, a fiery love, and solely out of
love, You have redeemed us although You have no need of us.

(Prayer 5.)

Catherine saw in the wounds of the risen Christ the proof
of this infinite love, ever alert to save us:

You also prepared another remedy, that is, keeping the marks of
His wounds in the body of the Word so that they may plead unceasingly before Your mercy for us. Yes, I have seen in Your light
that the ardor of Your love has willed this pleading. The wounds
are not effaced by the glory of His body; His blood remains scarlet,
and the glory of His body does not suffer any harm therefrom.

(Prayer 7.)

In cooperating with the redemption, to which her whole
life was devoted, Catherine never ceased to contemplate
God's love, a love so great that nothing created, not even the
passion suffered by Christ, can express it. For her, to become
a true apostle was to arrive, through the wound in Christ's
side, at "the secret of [His] heart," because that is where we
learn to love as Christ loves. This part of the *Dialogue*—
most of which, we must remember, is spoken by God—expresses clearly the idea that was one of Catherine's ruling
thoughts:

"They have come to the wound in [His] side, where they have found the secret of [His] heart, in which, through having held out the cup of their soul, they have known the baptism of water that draws all its virtue from [His] Blood. Where has the soul known the dignity of seeing itself united with and kneaded into the Blood of the Lamb in receiving holy baptism? In the wound in [His] side, where it experienced the fire of divine charity. That is what My Truth showed you, if you remember, when you asked Him, 'Alas, sweet immaculate Lamb, You were dead when Your side was opened. Why, then, did You will Your heart to be struck and broken?' And He, if you remember well, answered you, 'I had several reasons, but I am going to tell you the main one. It was because My desire toward the human race was infinite, while the torments and sufferings that I had endured were finite; and also because I could not show you, by means of finite things, all the love I had for you, since My love was infinite. Therefore, by showing you My open side, I wished you to see the secret of My heart so that you could see that I loved much more than I could show by My finite sufferings. In causing the blood and water to spurt [from My side], I showed you that you had received the holy baptism of water by virtue of [My] blood, and that is why My wound gave forth water and blood.' "

(Dialogue, Chap. 75.)

Meditation on Christ crucified revealed to the Saint His intention to gather together all men in the unity of His Mystical Body. She had learned this truth from the very beginning of her spiritual life and had received that light which St. Paul desired for the first Christians so that they might know how the all-powerful action which had raised Christ from the dead was working in them (see Eph. 1:15–23). Catherine understood that this divine power, which had raised the dead body of the Savior, to whom she was continuously united, was working in her. Christ had said to her:

63

"This life of the divine nature, united with My body, was hidden when it willed to be, and made its power burst forth when it so wished. But I have created you in My image and likeness; even more, by taking your nature I have made Myself like you. Consequently, I never cease striving to make you as much like Me as you are capable of being and I endeavor to renew in your soul, while you are on the way to heaven, all that has taken place in My body."

(*Life*, Part 1, Chap. 11.)

In addition, Catherine often uses the metaphor of grafting: the divine nature grafted on to the wild stock of human nature allows men to bear supernatural fruits capable of pleasing God.

Christ's Blood, the source of all fruitfulness, was confided to Holy Church, and it is in this perspective that Catherine contemplated the mystery of the Church. Throughout her correspondence she continually refers to this aspect of the Church, but one of the most beautiful passages on this subject occurs in her last letter to Blessed Raymond:

But just as no one can taste the beauty of God in the abyss of the Trinity without the mediation of this sweet Spouse [the Church] because everyone must pass through the door, which is Christ crucified—the door found only in the Church—I saw that this Spouse distributes life (and there is so much life in her that no one can do her to death); I saw that she gives strength and light, that no one can enfeeble or obscure her and that the fruit which she must bear, far from ever being lacking, always increases.

(Letter 371.)

Therefore, Catherine's inner vision of the apostolic soul centered upon the love that is God Himself, Father, Son and

Holy Spirit, manifesting itself in Christ the Savior and leading us to the Father by incorporating us into Christ. Leading all men to the Father through the Son was the work in which she was inspired to cooperate by spending herself to the last drop of her blood.

7. One with God

TO LOVE God is our whole life, the source of our merit, of our eternity and of the glory that we give to our Father. Moreover, the first and most urgent commandment is that we love God with our whole heart, our whole soul and with all our strength. The Incarnate Word knew that it was impossible that He should will otherwise: "I have come to cast fire upon the earth, and what will I but that it be kindled?" (Luke 12:49). He was raised up from the earth to draw all things to Himself, and the impulses of His grace, His precepts and the sacramental system are all faced toward developing the love of God in our souls, thus carrying out His divine will and establishing eternal harmony.

Catholic theologians give many proofs for these statements; but, in a world bewitched by fleeting passion, the mystics bear even greater witness to God's thirst for our love. With her special genius and grace, St. Catherine of Siena was one of the Church's most forceful preachers on divine love.

Nor is this surprising because the Divine Master used to speak at length to her about His thirst for men's love when He came to visit her every day in her narrow cell. In particular, after the vision of the exchange of hearts, she felt the Son of God's own heart beating in her breast. As we have seen, the Lord came to her and took away her own poor heart; then some days later, He returned to give her His heart, His own ardent divine heart. This grace, which is almost unique in the rich history of God's intimate dealings with His friends, is so well known that we need not stress it further.[1] Who can say how much this experience enriched Catherine's life? She herself described its effects to her confessor:

Father, can you not see that I am no longer the same person I was yesterday? I have been changed into someone else. . . . Father, if you only knew what I feel! I firmly believe that there is no heart so hard that it would not be softened, no pride so great that it would not be humbled, if it could experience what I feel within me. All that I can say is nothing compared with what I feel. . . . My soul is possessed by such joy, such jubilation, that I am greatly astonished it can remain in my body. . . . The ardor within me is so great that, after it, this material, outer fire seems to cool instead of burn. This ardor produces in my soul such a renewal of purity and humility that I seem to have gone back to the age of four or five. And my love for my neighbor is so enkindled that I would suffer death willingly and with great joy for anyone, no matter who he might be.

(*Life*, Part 2, Chap. 6.)

We can safely say that from then until her death every beat of her heart and every detail of her life was a conscious act of love. In her life, as in her soul, everything was to be done from love.

Filled as they are with references to divine love, Catherine's writings bear witness that her soul was enraptured with the

---

[1] We can compare this favor with the one which St. Margaret Mary Alacoque relates in her autobiography: "Our Lord asked me for my heart and placed it in His own adorable heart, where it was consumed in that ardent furnace, from which He then returned it to the place whence He had taken it. . . ." On another occasion, our Lord exchanged His heart for hers, saying: " 'I take such pleasure in seeing your heart that I wish to put Myself in its place and act as your heart.' And this was done so perceptibly that I could not doubt it."

splendors of charity. She saw first of all that only love meets the rightful sovereign demands of God: "I who am infinite therefore demand infinite actions, that is, an infinite desire to love" (*Dialogue*, Chap. 11).

Only one emotion gives us completely over to God:

Once the heart has been drawn to love its benefactor, the whole man is attracted—heart, soul and will, with all their spiritual aspirations—because these powers of the soul, which is spiritual, are drawn by love. The memory is drawn by the power of the Eternal Father and constrained to remember the benefits received from Him and to retain, out of the affection of love, the memory of them, and gratitude and acknowledgment for them. The intellect is raised toward the wisdom of the immolated Lamb in order to see in Him the fire of His charity, in which it acknowledges that God's judgments are just; it sees that all that God permits, prosperity or adversity, is given out of love and not out of hatred, and for this reason it receives and gathers in everything as a proof of love.

(Letter 259, to Tommaso d'Alviano.)

However, Catherine seemed to be even more impressed and almost fascinated by God's desire and actions: "Love was nailed to the cross because man was made from love and could not be better won than by love." She could not contain her amazement:

O folly of love! Did You need Your creature? Yes, I think You did, because You acted as if You were unable to live without it, although You are life itself and the source of all life, and although nothing can live without You.

(*Dialogue*, Chap. 153.)

From her desire to have Fra Giusto, the Prior of Mont'-Oliveto, share in her conviction, we get a further glimpse into the depths of her emotion: "Let us be zealous, since, as you see, it was because of this thirst that He is dying" (Letter 8). Christ's death attracts our love irresistibly: "How great is the danger and the shame of knowing that we are loved and of not loving in return!" she concludes in great distress (Letter 217, to the Prioress and the other Sisters of Santa Maria degli Angeli).

This theme of indebtedness, of necessity, obsessed her and, we can almost say, was an obstacle to her generosity and exquisite perceptiveness. Happily, however, she was to find in her neighbor a solace for her pain:

He has loved us without being loved, while we love Him because we are loved. He loves us freely, and we love Him out of obligation, because we are bound to love Him. . . . Long before He was loved, He loved us. Did He not create us in His own image and likeness?
(Letter 94, to Fra Matteo Tolomei.)

Catherine's realistic outlook also made her appreciate the infinitely precious advantages of this love, for when the soul is espoused by God it becomes divine. She often reverts to this theme: "Love transforms, making one Him who loves and him who is loved" (Letter 108, to Monna Giovanna di Capo, and to Francesca). Or again, "The fire of divine charity does for the soul what material fire does: it heats, purifies and converts things into itself" (Letter 109, to Gérard de Puy, Abbot of Marmoutier). She also considered the advantages of love in relation to eternity: "Let your soul be clothed in love, for it is with love that we enter eternal life" (Letter 72, to Romano, a linen weaver in the Bigallo company in Florence). And she quotes God as saying: "In My house there are many mansions, and I wish for nothing else but love" (*Dialogue*, Chap. 7).

Finally, Catherine also knew that only in God can our souls find repose, that everywhere else they will experience only disappointment and disquiet "because such is the condition of the soul. Infinite in its essence, it desires infinitely; it will never be satisfied until it is united with the infinite" (Letter 77, to William of England). God is love, and the soul, created by love, tends toward that love. In her own vivid way, Catherine explains this by having our Lord use a metaphor that has been described[2] as "not unworthy of the Gospel": "I am the fire and you are the sparks" (Letter 70, to Fra Bartolomeo Dominici). Or, as God expresses it in the *Dialogue*,

> "The soul cannot live without love; it always wishes to love something. It is totally impregnated with love because I have created it through love."
>
> (*Dialogue*, Chap. 51.)

In particular, her thoughts naturally reverted to the state of the perfect, for only the heights of sanctity draw generous souls onwards. In her confidences to Fra Raymond she often spoke of the state of the soul that loves God. She used to say

that such a soul no longer sees itself, that it no longer has any love for itself or for others, that it no longer remembers itself or any creature. . . . The soul that already sees its own nothingness and knows that its whole good lies in the Creator, completely forsakes itself and all its powers and every creature, immersing itself entirely in the Creator, who becomes for it the principal and only object of all its actions. It feels that it has found in Him all good and perfect happiness, and it no longer wishes to depart from Him in any way. This vision of love, which becomes clearer every day, so transforms the soul into God, as it were, that its thoughts, mind, heart and memory can no longer have any object except God and the things of

[2] Papini: *Storia della letteratura italiana* (Florence: Vallecchi, 1937), p. 422.

God. It sees itself and other creatures in God alone; only in God does it remember itself and others. A man who dives into the sea and swims underwater sees and touches only the water and the things in it. He sees nothing, touches nothing and feels nothing outside the water. If things outside the water are reflected in it, then he can see them, but only in the water, as far as they are visible in it, and in no other way. This, she used to say, is the proper and well-ordered love we ought to have for ourselves and for all creatures. There is never any error in this love because it is regulated by God. It never makes us desire anything outside God and consequently it always acts and develops within God.

(*Life*, Part 1, Chap. 10.)

When we gather together Catherine's views on this perfect love, we find that it has four main characteristics. It unceasingly aspires to the face-to-face vision of eternal beauty, and nothing on earth can satisfy it. It is generous, never recoiling from any task required in the service of God. It is self-sacrificing, having no resting place except in sacrifice. And it is fiery, ardently desiring the glory of God.

But imperfect love, on the contrary, still seeks itself. It may be tender, but it is still feeble, either because it is enticed by consolation or frightened by trials. To use Catherine's own typically energetic words, "It fail[s] at the moment of the cross" (Letter 94, to Fra Matteo Tolomei). It is more attached to the gift than to the giver, whereas true love finds rest only in the total gift of self, and its only symbol is the cross: "Let us love to the end, as Christ has loved us." By living only for Him and like Him, the soul becomes something that cannot be described without awe: "It becomes another self [with God] through a union of love" (*Dialogue*, Chap. 96).

With convictions so deep, she was bound to announce them to everyone. That was her gospel, and she had only one thing to say to Pope and sinner alike: "Remain in the sweet

71

and holy love of God." She knew nothing of that timidity that reserves the message of love for a narrow circle of chosen souls. God expects love and ever more love from every soul, whether it is mired in sin or soaring toward sanctity. Catherine never lost sight of this divine intent and she made it seem almost like anxiety on God's part. Of all the letters she wrote, perhaps the one to Bernabò Visconti is the most striking in this respect. Although Bernabò was one of the most powerful men in northern Italy and one of the most notorious tyrants of the fourteenth century, Catherine did not hesitate to speak to him about her favorite theme:

O very dear father, where then is the heart that is so obdurate, so hard, that it cannot be melted at the thought of the love and affection which the divine goodness has for it? Therefore, love, love! Know that you are loved when you can love no more, for it is in regarding Himself that God falls in love with the beauty of His creature, and, urged by the fire of His ardent charity, He desires to give us eternal life and the enjoyment of that infinite good which He enjoys in Himself. (O Ineffable Love, how well you knew how to prove your love when man lost grace through mortal sin, when he was deprived of it because he disobeyed You, O Lord.) Consider, father, the means that the mercy of the Holy Spirit has used to restore grace to men. Consider: the supreme greatness of God has taken on the servitude of our humanity and has abased itself so humbly that our pride must be confounded by it.

(Letter 28.)

Perhaps this wish to spread charity was the most salient feature of her apostolate in the world at large. The great danger of a secular life is a dispersal of effort, a forgetfulness of the final end because of preoccupation with the immediate demands of living. In such a life, there is no rule to bring unity into our efforts or to bear us along like a ship in which we have embarked. Again, the soul that wishes to become holy in the world must carry about with it the pain of love like an open, bleeding wound. Catherine knew this well because, as Stefano Maconi said (*Leggenda minore*, Part 2, Chap. 6), "ardent and all on fire with the love of God and her neighbor, she became almost like a seraph, constantly striving to fan the fire of love in others," wishing to pierce all hearts with her fiery sword.

8. As God First Loved Us

❖❖❖❖❖❖❖❖❖

THE beloved disciple, St. John, crushed beneath the weight
of Christ's immense love, looked for relief in the love
of his fellow men: "Beloved, if God has so loved us, we also
ought to love one another" (1 John 4:11). Catherine, bowed
beneath the greatness of the same love, had experienced the
same inclination to seek relief in the love of her neighbor. This,
too, was one of the characteristic traits of her mind and
doctrine:

How can we show Him a love like His, because although on the one
hand He asks it of us, on the other hand it is impossible for us to give
it to Him? I am going to tell you how—in the manner He Himself
has chosen. We ought to love Him generously and without any
regard for our own interests. That is, we ought to make ourselves
useful, not to Him—which we could not do, anyway—but to our
neighbor.

(Letter 94, to Fra Matteo Tolomei.)

Again she said:

God loves men to the highest degree, and if God's servants love them
spontaneously, it is because they see the love that God has for them.
The law of love is to love that which the beloved loves.

(Letter 16, to a great prelate.)

74

In another of her letters she teaches that our neighbor has been given to us as a means of showing the love we have for God. When our hearts are filled with love of, and desire for, God, they expand to love our neighbor with fraternal charity and not out of self-interest. "It is through our neighbor that we ought to love God and that we will show that we love Him" (Letter 254, to Pietro, son of Jacomo Attacusi de' Tolomei of Siena). In the *Dialogue,* God says: *to Catherine :*

> "I have loved you without being loved by you, before you existed. Love constrained Me even to create you in My own image and likeness. You cannot love Me in the same way but you ought to give this love to creatures by loving them without their loving you, by loving them without any spiritual or temporal self-interest, by loving them solely for the glory and praise of My name and because I love them."
>
> (*Dialogue,* Chap. 89.)

Whence did Catherine derive her profound understanding of this aspect of Christianity, which so many mystics leave unexplored? Perhaps she obtained it from that sense of solidarity which is the result of being reared in a large family and in the close-knit community of a city-state. As she herself put it:

> "Whether a person wills it or not, he is bound. Although he may deliberately wish to exempt himself from charity toward his neighbor, necessity binds him to it. . . . Your bodily members should make you blush for shame because they practice charity toward each other while you do not."
>
> (*Dialogue,* Chap. 148.)

Here in particular, divine guidance assisted nature, and an extraordinary grace begot in Catherine her great love for her fellow men. Only the gift of Christ can make us like Him. Catherine could not but be all afire with love for the poor when her Lord Himself appeared to her carrying the alms she had given that very day to particularly demanding beggars or when she saw Him miraculously multiplying the bread and wine she had given in charity. But the prodigies that occurred while she was tending the sick were even more wonderful still. The leprosy which she contracted while nursing an old woman named Cecca disappeared when her labor of devotion was ended and she had buried Cecca with her own hands. The pus which she drank to overcome her repulsion to the cancerous condition of a hateful old woman, who in addition slandered her shamefully, changed into a surpassingly sweet liquid. More than once our Lord allowed her to drink from the wound in His side, and she was allowed to see, and be thanked by, certain souls before they entered heaven.

But who would not become an apostle of charity if he could actually see those things whose reality we appreciate so little? Still, there is scarcely any need to point out that such extraordinary graces are only the palpable result of a spiritual reality and that it would be a mistake to overlook this essential fact. Yet there is in these graces a decisive and vitally important element which, moreover, throws into high relief something we often forget: namely, that every extraordinary grace presupposes heroic fidelity. God does not bestow His gifts lightly. The saints are saints only because they made the necessary effort.

There was in Siena another old woman who came to hate Catherine so much for her goodness and sanctity that the very sight of the young *Mantellata* and even the sound of her name infuriated her. Moreover, this woman never missed an opportunity to calumniate and curse the young saint. Catherine, acutely aware of this, did all she could by tactful service, humility and charity to win over her enemy but to no avail; her friendly overtures only met with contempt and sarcasm.

When Palmerina—that was the woman's name—fell ill and steadily grew weaker, Catherine hastened to her aid, treating her with even more kindness, affectionate attention and eager devotion. But Palmerina would not relent and seemed likely to go to her grave without the sacraments and still consumed with hatred. Catherine, however, persevered but only had the door shut in her face for her pains. To a heart less loving, less tenacious in its love and less resolute in its heroic desire to do good to those who wished it evil, all would have seemed lost. But when Catherine saw that she could not touch the dying woman's stony heart, she resolved instead to win over her divine Judge. She herself would pay whatever was needed to ransom this soul; she would save it from God's justice and turn it over to His mercy.

The struggle began, Catherine asking for grace for the culprit, our Lord apparently refusing it, and Catherine then reiterating her request. A whole day passed during which, contrary to all expectation, Palmerina's agony continued. Catherine remained adamant: she would not leave her cell until she had obtained mercy for the dying woman. Let the Master punish her for Palmerina's sins but let Him have mercy on the sinner. Two more days and nights went by while Catherine continued to beseech Him. Finally the Lord, having achieved His purpose of increasing still more her heroic charity, acceded to her request. She then hastened to the bedside of the dying woman, whose long agony had contradicted all the laws of nature and astonished those around her. But even more astonishing still were the joy and respect with which Palmerina received her whom she had hitherto hated so much and who had come unsummoned. A short while later, the sick woman died peacefully, reconciled with God and with Catherine.

Then, lifting the veil that hides the spiritual world from our eyes, Christ showed the Saint the soul she had just saved.

Although it had not yet entered heaven but possessed only the splendor bestowed on it by its creation by God and the grace of baptism, yet it was so beautiful that no human description could do it justice. To Catherine, our Lord said:

"Dearest daughter, see how, through you, I have retrieved this soul that was already lost. Does it not look very gracious and beautiful to you? Who, then, would not undergo any labor whatsoever to win so lovely a creature? If I, who am the Sovereign Beauty from whom all other beauty comes, was so enamored of the beauty of souls that I willed to come down on earth and shed My own Blood to redeem them, how much more ought you to work for one another so as not to allow such beautiful creatures to be lost! I showed you this soul to make you more fervent in procuring the salvation of every soul and to induce you to lead others to do this work, according to the grace that will be given you."

(*Life*, Part 2, Chap. 4.)

After this vision, Catherine asserted to Blessed Raymond:

Father, if you had seen the beauty of the rational soul, I have no doubt that you would be ready to undergo bodily death a hundred times over if that were possible, to save one soul. Nothing on this earth can compare with such beauty.

(*Ibid.*)

In the light of what she had seen she fully understood the meaning of God's words: "Love for Me and love for the neighbor are one and the same thing" (*Dialogue*, Chap. 7). Therefore she found God, whom she was seeking with all her strength, under the guise of her neighbor. In this she was aided by very great mystical graces which made the light of faith gleam brightly for her. Thus enlightened, she obviously loved her brethren for God's sake alone. But God became incarnate and therefore our love for Him reaches down to all our neighbor's weaknesses and failings, surrounding him with solicitude, respect, tenderness and care.

However, for the Christian, it is the soul that matters most because of its likeness to God and its eternal destiny. This was especially true of Catherine, whose vocation and particular grace were apostolic and whose love for her neighbor was therefore primarily a love for souls, a real passion and a holy obsession. She would have wished, if it were possible, to be placed in the very jaws of hell to prevent her brethren from falling into it. She once assured a Jew: "My soul longs to see you reach the light of holy baptism as a panting deer longs for running water" (Letter 15, to Consiglio). As the result of an extraordinary grace, she knew that, for the sake of sinners, she had been driven out of Paradise and set to wander through the world. Life had already left her body when our Lady appeared to her, saying:

> "Catherine, my daughter, do you see all this multitude of people following me? . . . You must make a choice. My Son wants you to go on living and wishes to give you all these people for eternal life in addition to those He has already given you, provided that your death be put off until another time. However, if you wish to die now, He will not give you those I have just shown you. Choose now whichever pleases you the most."

Catherine answered by making an act of abandonment to God's good pleasure. Then our Lady continued:

> "Be comforted now because my Son has given you all those I have shown you, in addition to those He gave you before. And as for you, He will call you to Him in another way when it will please Him."
>
> (*Fioretti*, p. 40.)

The memory of this vision made her say later:

79

Do you understand my love for sinners? They have cost me dear enough because the Lord drove me from Paradise on their account. Yet, as St. Paul said, the sinners that are to be saved are my glory, my crown and my joy.

(*Life*, Part 2, Chap. 6.)

When she had been restored to life and to her usual tasks, Catherine retained the indelible memory of this vision. The souls she had seen had cost her eternal life, and nothing short of their salvation could stifle the pangs of her regret. Indeed, her hunger for souls was capable of becoming so acute as to cause her death. To one of her correspondents she wrote: "I desire to see this hunger for the salvation of souls grow so much in you . . . that you will die of it!" (Letter 16, to a great prelate).

Her words recall those of Moses and St. Paul; and the drama of the Redemption echoed in her soul with all its moving poignancy. She continually spoke of hunger so great and desires so ardent that they were a torture that inspired her prayer and made it both humble and daring: "What good would eternal life be to me if I saw that Your people were in eternal death?" (*Dialogue*, Chap. 13). "I shall not rise from before Your face until I have obtained mercy! . . . Lord, I have not come to argue with Your justice but to ask mercy of You, O my Lord, and infinite clemency" (*Fioretti*, p. 72). Or as she declared more impressively still in the cry that revealed her close union with redeeming love: "I will it!"

Her love for souls gave her exhortations a unique note of strength and tenderness:

I, your poor mother, go everywhere seeking you and asking for you. I should like you to take upon your shoulders some of the sorrow and pity I feel for your soul. . . . Break this bond, and come, come, my dear child! I can well call you "dear," for you cost me so many tears, so much pain and perspiration!

> (Letter 45, to Francesco Malavolti of Siena.)

Yet the ardor of her desires did not beget disquiet or confusion in her or dim the clearness of her judgment, which remained wise with the wisdom of the love that inspired it. She knew how to be all things to all men, giving to each one the advice he needed; and because of a very special grace, the fervor of her prayer only sharpened her insight. She used to say:

When the servant of God prays His Divine Majesty very reverently, with great ardor and with the fervor of the charity which he has for the salvation of sinners, God gives him the grace to see with the eyes of his soul all those for whom he prays.

> (Fioretti, p. 19.)

Thus, with regard to understanding and humble service, she succeeded in "communicating with [her] neighbor," as she herself would say. Her love was not an abstract thing, for, while it did come from on high, it brought into play all the spontaneity and depth of her woman's heart. She had an especial love for children because of their innocence, and she sometimes used to say: "If propriety did not forbid it, I would hug them all the time."[1]

We find this deep affection especially in her dealings with her own spiritual "children," to whom she used to say: "I do not want you—indeed I forbid you—to suffer any need without telling me about it" (Leggenda minore); and her solicitude was so apparent that one of them could write: "I

[1] P. Lemonnyer: *Notre vie spirituelle à l'école de sainte Catherine de Sienne* (Ed. Vie Spirituelle), p. 51.

assert and truly believe that our loving *Mamma* is indeed a mother" (*Ibid.*, p. 275). In reality there is no better word than "mother" to express the purity, patience and sensitivity of Catherine's love. Moreover, the group which gathered around her came to form a real family with all the freedom, warmth and depth of affection the term implies. Even after an interval of six centuries we can recapture the charm of the group from some of their letters that have escaped the destruction of time. Here are a few of many examples: "Your peace is as dear to me as the peace of my own soul" (*Ibid.*, p. 299) ; "Remember me to all our poor little family . . . recalling that its head especially and all its members are rooted deep in my heart" (*Ibid.*, p. 277) ; and the following spontaneous note, showing the gaiety and family spirit that reigned among the "children": "Messer Matteo himself nearly died laughing. I beg you to tell *Mamma* about it so that she will know how things are going. Answer quickly so that I shall not lose hope, even though you tell me only trifles; it would be a comfort to me to receive anything" (*Ibid.*, p. 281).

Even after the Saint's death, the family bonds remained intact, if we are to judge by greetings such as: "Sweetest brother, most cordially loved in Christ and in the holy memory [of Catherine]" (*Ibid.*, p. 298). That was one of the articles of the testament which their *dolce mamma* had left to her spiritual children: "Love one another, my dearest children; wish each other well!" (*Life*, Part 3, Chap. 4).

9. Progress in Charity

IF WE confined ourselves to what we have just said, we should be far from having explained all of Catherine's doctrine on charity. Like every mystic, she yearned for the heights of divine union, yet she carried in her heart the anguish of the world and longed to save her fellow men, with whom she lived in closest contact. Constantly aware of the oneness and the extensions of charity, she never for a moment lost sight of the amplitude that it must have. But when she dictated to her secretaries, she spoke spontaneously and from a full heart, so that we are torn between desire to follow the grand sweep of her thought and regret at leaving aside any part of her treasury of doctrine.

Whenever Catherine speaks of charity, we feel that she takes her place over against that divine love that wills to give itself to a world tragically overrun by sin because of the infidelity of Christ's own disciples. The second book of the *Dialogue*, in which she sets forth her teaching on the progress of charity, opens with this mysterious contrast between God, who has done everything possible for mankind, and man himself, who responds to God's love by doing all the evil in his power. Here we are irresistibly reminded of the Bible passage in which the prophet Micheas shows God summoning

His people in judgment before the mountains and hills. But in the *Dialogue*, God is thinking only of showing mercy, and His mercy will not be brought about by means of plagues or other external events but by His servants. That is what lends originality to her teaching, in which many of the basic elements are classical in the schools of spirituality.

Before humanity there stretches a bridge leading from earth to heaven, uniting the human with the divine, resting on the earth but also reaching heaven. This bridge is Christ, God who became man to unite these two extremes and to permit us to reach Him who loves us so greatly that He seems unable to do without us. Under the bridge thunders the river that sweeps to perdition those who will to go there by refusing to cross over by the bridge of salvation.

The first ones who seem about to set out across the bridge are those who have turned away from sin because of servile fear. They seem to have turned away from evil, but their hearts are still attached to it. These have not yet set foot on the bridge itself, and if they remain where they are, they will not persevere in their sorrow and in their efforts to avoid sin. They really do not desire what is good but are motivated only by self-love. That is why, when confronted with difficulties or when tempted, they think solely of their own pleasure or convenience and are easily overcome and look back: "Without perseverance no one attains the goal for which he has begun to strive" (*Dialogue*, Chap. 49); "All this happens solely because the root of self-love has not been completely removed from their souls. . . . That is why they do not persevere" (*Ibid.*). Or it can easily happen that, because they dislike effort, they become presumptuous and abuse God's mercy by remaining in their sins. Perseverance demands that the soul gather its forces to keep advancing along the path of goodness and to set out resolutely across the bridge.

Only through love can we set foot on and cross over the bridge: if we are motivated merely by servile fear we cannot even begin the journey. To Catherine's mind, the first stage of the bridge is represented by Christ's wounded feet, at which imperfect love stops and which the soul reaches by casting off its affection for sin. This symbolism was very popular in the Middle Ages, when Christ's feet were regarded as a figure of the soul's progress and hence of its love, while His hands naturally represented the good works that each Christian did.

We cannot come to Christ's feet without a true desire for what is good: "Therefore we must thirst because only those who thirst have been invited." No effort on our part is effective unless we truly desire what is good. Furthermore, we cannot act as isolated units, cut off from our neighbor by lack of charity: "He who is alone, that is, he who is shut up in self-love, does not count as regards My truth, nor do I accept him," for the divine promise is restricted to "those who are many" (*Dialogue*, Chap. 54).

It is thus that the Christian gradually attains the joy of love.

> "It is very easy because nothing is as easy and pleasant as love. And what I ask of you is nothing but love and affection for Me and your neighbor. That is possible at all times, in every place and in every human circumstance by loving and fearing everything for the praise and glory of My name."
>
> (*Dialogue*, Chap. 55.)

By showing us the reward which God has promised to His sons, faith strengthens our efforts at this stage to unify our soul's forces, helping us to persevere and make progress. But we still have very many imperfections; we are still mercenary and cleave to God out of self-interest, as is proved by the way we act in times of trial.

Catherine uses a charming simile to describe this state of soul. A man who has a garden loves to spend his time there and is so enthusiastic about cultivating it that he sincerely believes he likes gardening work. But if he loses his garden, he soon realizes that it is not the work involved in gardening that he likes—for he could find that easily enough elsewhere—but rather that he simply enjoys being in his own garden. It is the same with those trials which show that we are seeking ourselves in serving God and are not working solely for Him.

By alternating spiritual consolations with aridity, Providence leads the soul to a pure love that seeks only God in God. Catherine decried the grave harm that the soul suffers from every undue attachment to spiritual things, because thereby the soul is bound to a past which it would like to relive or because it is rendered unwilling to submit to the guidance of the Holy Spirit. The soul tries to "lay down the law" to the Holy Spirit because it wants to serve Him in its own way. She then lamented the danger run by those who, under the pretext of safeguarding their peace and their piety, turn away from the work of the apostolate. Referring to the case of the hermit who refused to leave the solitude of his forest and come to Rome, she wrote: "If merely changing from one place to another breaks the bond between the soul and the Holy Spirit, then that bond was very weak to begin with" (Letter 328, to Fra Antonio da Nizza).

Here we must stress a point of doctrine proper to St. Catherine. Convinced as she was of the unity between love of God and love of neighbor for God's sake, she returned again and again to what she considered the clearest sign that love was still imperfect. When someone we love hurts or deceives us, leaves us for another, seems to prefer someone else to us, or has different views from ours, what is our reaction? If that reaction is inspired by God and is free from all self-interest, we know that our love for the other person borders on perfection. But if we react by feeling hurt, by being sad or discouraged, by taking offense or by regretting our apparently fruitless devotion and by brooding on similar thoughts, we show how imperfect our love was. If our hearts had been filled with God, they would not be left empty so easily.

The Saint often returns to this thought, which can give an apostolic soul a keen insight into its own and others' motives. Catherine's own formulation of this principle appears in a letter to Fra Geronimo da Siena:

What means do we possess for making [our love] perfect? I shall show you, my beloved son, no other means except that which Supreme Truth once revealed to one of His servants in these words: "My beloved daughter, I do not want you to act like one who draws a vessel full of water from the fountain and drinks it after he has drawn it. Thus the vessel remains empty—a fact which he does not realize. I wish that in filling the vessel of your soul, in becoming, by your love and affection, one with him whom you love for My sake, you do not take him away from Me, who am the fountain of living water. Rather, out of love for Me, keep the creature whom you love, like a vessel in the water. In that way, neither you nor he will ever be empty, but on the contrary both of you will always be full of divine grace and of the fire of divine love." Then you will no more experience either anger or sorrow, because he who loves will not be troubled by any change or remoteness he may notice if he sees also that the one he loves is still living a life full of mature and genuine virtues, for he loves the beloved for God's sake and not out of self-interest. Rather he would in fact experience a sweet and holy tenderness if he saw that he was abandoned by the one he loves. That is the rule and the method you should follow to be perfect.

(Letter 52.)

In another context, when writing to Niccolò the Poor, a

hermit of Florence, Catherine concluded her letter by recommending him

to provide for the spiritual and temporal needs of our neighbor without ever thinking about the profit or consolation you may derive therefrom here on earth. Simply love him and help him because God loves him. Thus you will practice love of neighbor according to God's commandment and my wishes.

(Letter 78.)

Guided by faith, the soul that strives to love God for Himself must learn to give itself to Him so that it may perceive that everything comes from Him and that not a leaf falls from a tree outside the order of His Providence. Such a soul should receive lovingly what God gives out of love, especially in all that concerns prayer, and it should derive profit from everything that happens to it, thus cooperating with God's intention of uniting His followers with Him.

By constant prayer we shall come to see God's love more and more clearly and learn to love Him for Himself and our neighbor for His sake. Then we shall have access to the wound in our Lord's side.

The Sacred Heart is the second stage on the bridge over which we must cross to attain eternal life, a stage reserved for those who love God for Himself and who have received the secret of His heart:

"I shall then love them like sons because I love as I am loved. If a person loves Me with servile love, I give him his due but I do not show Myself to him, for secrets are shared only with a friend who has become one with oneself. . . . I shall manifest Myself, and we shall dwell together." That is what a well-loved friend means—two bodies but only one soul in love—for the one who loves becomes the thing loved. If two friends form but one soul, there are no longer any secrets. That is why my Truth said: "I shall come and we shall dwell together." This is the plain truth.

(Dialogue, Chap. 60.)

The characteristic feature of this state seems to be the discovery of God's love in Christ, an immense love which embraces the whole of humanity and calls it to Him but which is more personal for each soul the more docilely each one surrenders himself to it. We have already quoted Catherine's beautiful words describing how the wound in Christ's side visibly and palpably reveals His infinite, invisible love. It is from His heart that His Blood springs, and, according to Catherine, it is thence also comes this mystery of His love. Furthermore, this state of soul is inseparable from the next stage of development, in somewhat the same way as love of neighbor is inseparable from love of God. Here we find the vital principle of Catherine's whole personality:

"I say that filial love is perfect because the creature that experiences this love receives My heritage from Me, the Eternal Father, because filial love includes the love of a friend who, as I have already told you, from being a friend has become a son."

(Dialogue, Chap. 72.)

The next stage, Christ's mouth, promises the kiss of peace and repose, but we must not forget that that same mouth tasted gall and vinegar. Here, the creature finds an inner unity because all the powers of its soul now cling to God for His sake alone. The loving soul

"will show that it has reached the state of perfection. Through where has it passed? Through the heart, that is, through the memory of the Blood where it found, as it were, a second baptism and where it renounced every imperfect love as a result of the knowledge it drew from this heartfelt love by seeing, tasting and experiencing the fire of My charity. Souls such as this, therefore, have arrived at the mouth, and that is why they prove it by acting like a mouth."

(*Dialogue*, Chap. 76.)

Catherine then repeats her usual metaphors: the mouth speaks to God, or it speaks to man about God, it tastes, and it chews, satisfying its hunger at the table of the cross, nourishing itself on the glory of God and the salvation of souls. Her metaphor is strained, it is true, yet it does not obscure the ideal proposed and promised to anyone who becomes united to God. The contrast between God, whom such a person tastes interiorly, and the sin of the world, of which he is a witness, should increase his desire. To Catherine, communing with Christ necessarily means sharing in His desires and, consequently, in His works to build up His Mystical Body. This state of union is marked by a readiness to serve God as He wishes to be served, without taking account of one's personal tastes, which have been burned away in Him who is the "Fire, which consumes the sacrifice of one's desires. . . ."

"[Such souls] serve Me courageously by forgetting themselves. No matter how they have to spend their lives and their allotted time, if it is for My glory, they are joyful and they find rest and peace of mind. Why is this? It is because they do not choose to serve in their own way but in Mine. That is why they are always ready. . . . They detest sin and respect everything apart from it."

(*Dialogue*, Chaps. 76 and 77.)

With them, everything is prayer and repose in God. Among friends, gifts do not count but rather the friends themselves. That is the way it is with these sons of God, especially because, since the Incarnation, they find the Giver in His gifts.

"The coal in the furnace has become fire and cannot be with-

90

drawn. Those souls that are plunged in the fire of My love, of whom nothing remains outside of Me, and who no longer have any will of their own but who are all on fire with Me—no one can seize such souls and withdraw them from Me and My grace because they have become one with Me and I with them."

(*Dialogue*, Chap. 78.)

It is quite clear, then, that, for Catherine, conformity with Christ and the transformation of man's will into His are a supremely active process. This transformation gives rise to the torment suffered by him who tries to please God, and, far from being a period of inaction, is one of intense effort. But this effort is in fact true repose because it unites the soul ever more closely with God; and while Catherine speaks about the Table at which we should nourish ourselves, she also refers to the bed upon which the soul can rest.

The soul that has already received the pledges of its divine inheritance no longer loses the sense of God's presence, which, however, only serves to make it more acutely aware of the infinite difference between union with God on earth and union with Him in heaven: "Once the soul has been raised to this perfect union, it desires only to see Me and to see glory and praise rendered to Me" (*Dialogue*, Chap. 4).

Nothing further then remains for the soul but to have its yearning for God satisfied, and this unfulfilled desire is the only obstacle that remains before it can immerse itself in the ocean of peace. Then "it cannot suffer pain but feels rather compassion without pain, loving sinners and begging Me out of love to show mercy to the world" (*Dialogue*, Chap. 82).

Catherine never forgot that on the heights of perfection charity assumes its full dimensions, that we cannot possess God without desiring His glory, and that perfect love necessarily means perfect desire to see Him loved.

91

10. Love of Neighbor

❖❖❖❖❖❖❖❖

ONE of the most marked characteristics of Catherine's mind was undoubtedly her realism or, if you will, her grasp of truth. She could not conceive how any love could be real and yet not change one's whole life. Hence came her basic principle: Give glory to God, and help your neighbor.

She learned from Christ crucified to allow herself to be devoured by thirst for the glory of God. This is the lesson she is trying to impart when she speaks of learning from Christ to sit down with Him at the table of the cross and nourish oneself there with God's glory. Hunger and thirst for the glory of God were the inspiration of her whole life. When she spoke about love of peace, about the war that must be waged on war, when she spoke about justice or about the wretchedness of the prostitute from Perugia, she was taking God's point of view, and this is what gave such insight, energy and zeal to her activities.

That is not the least of the lessons which the Saint has to teach modern apostles who, without realizing it, sometimes try to foster outside of Christ those convictions that should in reality be the fruits of Christ the Vine, fruits which He wishes to give through His apostles to a world that is dying for lack of them.

Action derives its value from this relationship with God, and only from it: "I am the Infinite; I look for infinite works— that is, those inspired by a boundless love." This holds good for everything, even Christ's Passion:

He punishes in Himself our iniquities; His body bears them and His will expiates them. With the will of the divine power that is in Him, He sacrifices His Blood to the Father, and thus His sacrifice is accepted.

(Letter 259, to Tommaso d'Alviano.)

Even more, for Catherine, referring everything to the glory of God (which results from true love alone) is the only motive capable of producing action because, as she herself vividly writes, lack of it "cuts off the arms of holy desire." Without this motive, we quickly become lazy and negligent; lack of true love of God makes us an easy prey to self-love and to the fear of making any effort, to worry lest we displease others, to taking pains to avoid discomfort and fatigue, and to self-serving egoism.

With this in mind, she did not hesitate to write to a cardinal:

I am sure that if you raise the eyes of your mind to see what [the Church] needs (now, both spiritually and temporally), you will act with solicitude and without any fear or negligence. If a soul is a victim of servile fear, none of its acts can be perfect. No matter how it may be situated, it finds that it is powerless in small matters as well as in important ones, and it cannot bring to perfection what it has begun. O how dangerous this fear is! It cuts off the arms of holy desire; it blinds a man by not allowing him to know or see the truth, for this fear comes from the blindness induced by self-love.

(Letter 11, to Peter, Cardinal of Ostia.)

Such wisdom as this is acquired only on the cross and by reading the book of life which is Christ Himself:

Therefore, since self-love and this inordinate fear are so dangerous, we must flee them. We must fix the eyes of our mind on this reality— the spotless Lamb who is our rule and our doctrine and whom we must follow . . . and who, in short, is Love and Truth Itself. He seeks only the glory of His Father and our salvation. He feared neither the Jews nor persecution nor the malice of demons nor shame nor mockery nor insults; and, finally, He did not fear the ignominious death on the cross. We are the pupils in this mild and gentle school. Therefore, dearest father, I wish that, with great solicitude and gentle prudence, you will open the eyes of your mind, on this earth, upon this book of life that teaches us so mild and gentle a doctrine. And do not busy yourself with anything except loving God, saving souls and serving the sweet Spouse of Christ.

(*Ibid.*)

When Catherine contemplated the whole mystery of the cross, she could not but see in it the expression of an infinite desire that no act or suffering could satisfy:

I am writing to you . . . with the desire to see you . . . imitating the Sweet Supreme Truth, whose hunger and thirst for our salvation is so great that He is dying of it. . . . O inestimable and sweetest Charity! . . . I am not surprised that Your love was infinite and Your torment finite, for the cross of desire was heavier than the cross of Your body.

(Letter 16, to a great prelate.)

Realist that she was, Catherine was no less rigorous in the application of the second part of her principle. To her way of thinking, the indisputable sign of a true intention to give glory to God is devotion to the neighbor, a devotion that extends both to the spiritual and the temporal. Here is how she expounded her doctrine in the *Dialogue*:

"[Virtue] is first conceived by love, is put to the proof by the neighbor and is brought forth for him. If virtue did not show itself and did not burst forth at the moment of need, in the presence of men, it would be false to say that it had been conceived. Have I not already said in effect to you that there can be no perfect, fruitful virtue without the neighbor? It is the same with a woman who has conceived a son in her womb, but if she does not give birth to him, if she does not have him be seen by the eyes of the world, her husband cannot consider himself a father. That is how it is with Me, who am the spouse of the soul. If the soul does not, in love of the neighbor, give birth to the son which is virtue, and does not show him [the son] as it should, in general and in particular, I say that it has not truly conceived virtue in itself."

(*Dialogue*, Chap. 11.)

In fact, it is impossible to love God without also being led to love the neighbor truly; and it was Catherine's mission to reiterate this truth. This is the heart of Christianity because the union between God and man is one of the consequences of the Incarnation. That is why, whatever we do for the least of Christ's brethren, we do for Him. That is why the persecution of Christians is the persecution of Christ Himself, a doctrine so basic that it was taught to St. Paul at the very instant of his conversion (see *Dialogue*, Chap. 64). Of all the mystics, St. Catherine in particular seems to have had the special mission of proclaiming the essential connection between love of God and love of neighbor. The following passage from the *Dialogue*, which, as we saw, she dictated not long before her death, repeats the doctrine which she had unceasingly taught all her life:

"Since [the soul] truly loves Me, it also truly serves its neighbor. It cannot be otherwise because love for Me and love of the neighbor are one and the same thing; the more the soul loves Me, the more it loves its neighbor because love of him proceeds from love of Me. This is the means I have offered you so that you may practice virtue and may experience it in yourself because, since you cannot profit Me in any way, you should be helpful to your neighbor. This will be the sign that you possess Me by grace in your soul. You will have your neighbor share in your many devout prayers, with sweet, loving desire, seeking My glory and the salvation of souls.

"The soul enamored of My truth never ceases to make itself useful, in general and in particular, to a greater or lesser degree, according to the dispositions of him who is to benefit by it and according to the fervor of him who offers it. I said this to you already when I explained above that chastisement alone, unaccompanied by desire, is insufficient to expiate a fault.

"When this love of union with Me has disposed the soul to love its neighbor and to extend its desire to include the salvation of the world in general, then the soul, having been rendered useful to itself by conceiving virtue which gives it the life of grace, exercises its ingenuity to see to the needs of each of its neighbors in particular. It then gives aid to those near it according to the different graces that I have granted it so that it may dispense them. It will teach some by word, will give advice to others, and by example will be a model for living. Each one is bound to edify his neighbor by a good, holy and upright life.

"These are the virtues that are born of love of neighbor, and there are so many others that you could not name them all, but I cannot speak to you about all of them. . . . Love of neighbor is perfected in love for Me. When love of neighbor is attained, the law is observed. He who is bound by love does everything it is possible to do."

(*Dialogue*, Chap. 7.)

In this service of the neighbor, whether by praying for

him or by rendering him spiritual or material assistance, Catherine most feared hypocrisy and empty words. That was one of the truths engraved on her heart: "I am He who delights in few words and many acts" (*Dialogue*, Chap. 11).

11. The Achievements of Love

❖❖❖❖❖❖❖❖❖

THE controversy about action and contemplation, the debate between Martha and Mary, is an ancient one which our Lord really did not settle, leaving it instead to each individual's love to solve. He did not reproach Martha for being diligent in serving Him but only for becoming perturbed and losing sight of the one thing necessary. Nor did He praise Mary for her inaction but only for her loving attention.

Catherine's solution to the problem was to do Martha's work with Mary's spirit. She herself attained this ideal, not by her own efforts, but by a victory of grace which expanded her soul and heart. Perhaps more evidently than any other saint, she put into practice St. Thomas' principle that action should be combined with contemplation "as an addition and not as a subtraction."

Raymond tells us how she came to leave her life as a recluse in order to enter on an apostolic career. It is evident that he uses some literary color to embellish his description but we can scarcely doubt that his account is fundamentally factual and is based on Catherine's own confidences to him, for it would be hard even to imagine such an unlikely beginning for so extraordinary a life. The unexpected appearance of a mere human endowed with divine mercy is like a trumpet call to which all the wretchedness of the world responds.

After a period of three years spent in absolute solitude, during which she was enriched with the most extraordinary mystical experiences and which she spent in ridding herself of all the material restrictions of human life, Catherine one day received this command: "Go, it is dinner time, and the members of your family are about to sit down at table. Go and join them, and then come back to me." When she heard this order, she broke out into sobs and tears, saying:

"O my Lord, greatest joy of my heart, why are You sending me away? If I have offended Your Majesty, let my body be punished here at Your feet and I will willingly help You do it. But do not allow me to be afflicted with a pain as great as that of being separated from You, O my supremely beloved Spouse, no matter what or how short this separation may be. What interest have I in eating? I have a food to eat which is unknown to those whom You are commanding me to join. Does man live by bread alone? Is it not by the word coming from Your mouth that every soul in this world will be made to live? As You know, I fled all companionship so that I might find You, my Lord and my God. Now that I have found You, thanks to Your mercy; now that You have deigned so graciously to give me the happiness of possessing You, I cannot abandon such an incomparable treasure and become involved once more in human affairs. My ignorance would once again increase, and, by letting myself slip little by little, I would finally deserve to be cast off by You. Never, Lord, never will Your infinite goodness command me or anyone else to do anything that could separate our souls from it."

These, and many others of the same kind, were the virgin's words; but her sobs said more than her voice, as she prostrated herself at the feet of the Lord. To her He replied: "Be calm, gentle daughter, for that is the way in which you must fulfill all justice and permit My grace to bear its fruits, not only in you, but also in others. I have no intention of separating you from Me in any way, but I want you to use the love of your neighbor to unite yourself more strongly to Me. You know that My precept of love is twofold—love of Me and love of neighbor. In these, I emphasize, are contained the Law and the prophets. I want you to fulfill the justice of these two precepts, to walk on two feet and not on one alone, to have two wings with which to fly to heaven. You must remember that it was I who sowed in your soul and watered there the seed of zeal for the salvation of men which has been growing since your infancy. This zeal was such that you wanted to pass yourself off as a man and go to a place where you were not known so that you might enter the Order of Preachers and thus be able to make yourself useful to souls. The reason why you so greatly desired the habit that you are wearing now was that you had a very special love for My faithful servant, Dominic, who began his work above all for the salvation of souls. Why then are you astonished and why do you complain when I lead you to do a task which you have so greatly desired since the first years of your life?" Somewhat consoled by the Lord's words, Catherine replied after the example of the Blessed Virgin Mary: "How shall this be done?" The Lord answered: "As My goodness shall dispose and ordain." And the Saint, like a faithful disciple imitating her Master, continued: "May Your will and not mine be done in all things!"

(*Life*, Part 2, Chap. 1.)

Thus thrust out into the world, Catherine went to take her place in the life of her family. But this small beginning quickly grew into something very much greater: first, charitable works among the sick and those in prison—the most repulsive cases, she believed, being reserved for her by God: "The virgin used to say . . . that these, her neighbors, were her especial joy and her only glory" (*Leggenda minore*, Part 2, Chap. 6); then social and civic work in cities and states; and finally, her extraordinary mission in the Church itself, even to the extent of being instrumental in bringing about the

Sovereign Pontiff's return from Avignon to Rome. In fact, it is difficult to estimate the scope of her work, so immense did it become. Yet despite her wide-ranging activities, the ties of affection that bound together her spiritual family did not slacken: in Avignon she had twenty-three disciples with her; in Rome she had twenty-four, and on some days as many as forty; and like a real mother and head of a family, she concerned herself about each of them and all their affairs. As we have already said, Raymond tells us that sinners thronged around her as if summoned by an invisible trumpet, and that so many were converted by her great charity that three confessors were in continuous demand to hear their confessions, receive their repentance and absolve them in the name of Christ. And we have seen that, to make it easier for these sinners to become reconciled with God, Pope Gregory XI, who had provided the confessors in the first place, also granted them very liberal faculties for absolution.

But that was not all. Catherine had in addition many absent friends, as well as all those who, without ever having seen her, still had recourse to her. Then, too, there were important public affairs to be settled, particularly the problems of the Church. At the time of the schism, her little room on the Via di Papa resembled the office of a ministry of state. There she had to dictate to three or four secretaries at a time, a practice in which she resembled the great men of action and which enables us to glimpse the extraordinary nature and scope of her work. Yet she did not cease to be the great contemplative to whom nothing mattered but the vision of God and whose whole strength reached out toward a union of love with Him. How did she do it? How was she able to reconcile these opposing tendencies? How did she solve the problem that has sharply vexed the conscience of every Christian forced to live in the clamor of the world?

In reality, it was no problem to her because, for her, contemplation and action were one and the same expression of love of God; every form of interior or exterior activity was a work of love and the fulfillment of her desires. Her contemplation led to action, and her activity was entirely contemplative. That was her way of being a Dominican and of leading the "mixed" life, in which contemplation and action are combined in a harmonious unit, as is the case with the angels, whose serene, clear vision of God is not disturbed by the missions which He assigns to them and whose contemplation is always the motive and the measure of their activity.

St. Catherine's contemplation was active. She never lost sight of the fact that the interior life alone is the soul of the apostolate; and she, better than anyone else, was aware of the nothingness and sterility of deeds done without love:

I am writing to you with the ardent desire to see you transformed in the fire of the most fervent charity so that you may be a vessel of election capable of carrying the word of God, in accordance with His great designs, into the presence of our sweet "Christ on earth," and so that you may succeed in setting his heart on fire. . . . I want you to extend these desires to the Mystical Body of Holy Church, for the glory of God and the salvation of every creature. . . . In doing this, your works and words will be like an arrow taken from the fire when well alight and then shot from the bow to set fire to everything it touches.

(Letter 192, to Neri di Landoccio.)

Her prayer and self-immolation supported her apostolic action, and her mission was so extensive because her immolation was so great. God entrusts His missions to souls in terms of their love, as is indicated by the incident in the Gospel where Christ first tested St. Peter's love before giving His sheep into his care (John 21:15-17). Even more, contemplation would seem incomplete if it did not fulfill itself in action. Catherine was granted the gift of self-expression so that her heart would not burst under the pressure of the fire that burned in it, as she herself relates: "The Lord gave me the gift of writing in order that when I came down from the heights I should have some way to pour out my heart so that it would not burst" (Letter 272, to Raymond of Capua).

In another context she praised the value which love imparts to every act:

[Divine charity] acts unceasingly and never grows weary. It is like the usurer who is always earning money with the mere passage of time: he is earning while he sleeps; he is earning while he eats; whatever he does, he is earning and never loses time. But it is not the usurer himself who is earning; rather it is the treasure of time that is bearing fruit. That is the way it is with the spouse who loves Christ, when she is on fire with divine charity: she is always earning and is never idle; while she sleeps, charity goes on working; whether she eats or sleeps or stays awake, she profits from everything.

(Letter 108, to Monna Giovanna di Capo and to Francesca.)

"The soul that loves God wants to see Him loved by the whole world" (Letter 263, to Monna Montagna). It is striking to see the place the misery of the world and the sins and wretchedness of men have in Catherine's sublime conversations with God, who spoke of them to her, His "beloved daughter." Just as Joan of Arc's voices were to speak to her about the dangers to her country so as to rouse her generosity, so, too, in order to make Catherine an apostle, God in His mercy revealed to her the great misery existing in the kingdom of souls and the leprosy that disfigured even the face of the Church. In this way He wished to "increase her desires to the point of anguish," and to spur on her efforts. From these ecstatic colloquies were born her bold enterprises and unflagging devotion.

Catherine's action was contemplative. She was certainly active, and we have seen the variety and scope of her works from household cares to her mission in the Church, all of which, however, only served to unite her more closely to God, as He had promised. She condemned the charity that "conceives" without "giving birth," and she was suspicious of a devotion that is lost when one simply changes from one place to another (see Letter 328, to Fra Antonio da Nizza), for God is not constrained to give Himself only in silence and solitude. Very much to the contrary, Catherine believed that we fly more quickly toward heaven with two wings—love of God and love of neighbor—than with only the one.

Yet she held that action must be the expression and, as it were, the incarnation of interior love, and that charity, not a mere urge to speak or an itch to be doing something, must be the principle of action. She never undertook any work except under the pressure of her zeal for the glory of God: were it not for this spur, she would never have left the repose of contemplation and the silence of her cell.

Charity must regulate and animate all our activities; as kindling in the flames, the wood of our actions must be turned into the fire of love. That is one of the dominant traits of Catherine's spiritual doctrine. She herself remained interiorly alert to catch Christ's voice, acting only upon His orders given by an inner inspiration, transmitted by obedience or indicated by Providence, so much so that the scholarly William Flete called her "the instrument of the Holy Spirit": "Inspired by this spirit, she corrected all disorderly speech so effectively and so gently that no one could gainsay her" (*Leggenda minore*, Part 1, Chap. 6). Hence came also the transparent uprightness of all her acts: "She did not seek to please, nor did she fear to displease" (*Fioretti*, p. 126), but simply spoke the truth. She willingly risked her reputation in order to help a poor person, preferring to walk through the streets without a cloak, as the prostitutes did, rather than without charity; and her firm attitude toward the nobles and even toward the Pope himself undoubtedly sprang from the same source.

She never indulged in idle chatter but rather spoke constantly about God and the things that lead us to Him; then "her face was like a seraph's because, due to the fullness of her heart, her lips spoke of that which burned within her" (*Leggenda minore*, Part 1, Chap. 6). "Everyone who approached her came away better and more enlightened" (Office of the Saint). She has been compared to the sun, from whose heat no one can escape; but we can derive a more accurate idea of her influence from this preface to her prayer in which, to obtain more graces from God, she recalls one which she has already received: "Lord, I shall not leave Your feet or Your presence as long as Your goodness does not give me what I desire, as long as You are not pleased to do what I wish" (Caffarini, *Supplemento*, Part 2, Chap. 3).

Events often turned out like this, as for instance in the case of Nanni di Ser Vanni. As we have seen, Nanni was a violent, vengeful man with blood on his hands and deadly hatred in his heart for four of his enemies. Very much against his will, he came to see Catherine, and, although she greeted him "with heavenly charity," he remained unmoved. First, using her powers of persuasion, she tried to make him promise to mend his ways, but when he would not give in, she withdrew within herself to pray in silence and recollection. Finally he relented somewhat by forgiving one of his four enemies out of courtesy to Catherine. But once the peace of Christ had gained entrance through this crack in his stubbornness, it went on to conquer him so completely that he broke into tears and poured out his sins to Catherine. Then he went to confession to Blessed Raymond and received absolution. Neither here nor anywhere else did Catherine seek her own glory but lived instead by the maxim which was often on her lips: "We must give the flowers—that is, the glory—to God, and the fruits [our services] to our neighbor." In one of her letters to Raymond, she expresses herself more fully on this subject:

In this way we nourish ourselves on souls for the glory of God. In order to snatch them from the hands of the demon, we would deliver ourselves over to death. Out of zeal we steal time from ourselves; that is to say, we refuse ourselves the time to enjoy certain consolations, whether new or old, and we give everything to our neighbor. That is why when a pious woman cried out, "My God, what do You wish me to do?" she received the reply: "Give glory to Me and your services to your neighbor."

(Letter 104, to Raymond of Capua.)

Moreover, Catherine took care that external activity never diminished the inner flame. Even while she was still quite young, she recognized this danger, so that when her parents tried to thwart her vocation by overwhelming her with work and depriving her of solitude, she had recourse to a pious fiction, making believe that she saw and served Christ in her father, the Blessed Virgin in her mother, and the Apostles and the holy women in her brothers and sisters.

In later years, the thought of the Precious Blood filled her whole mind; in it she lived, breathed, acted, wrote and spoke, experiencing a divine intoxication of love which ensured that her activity lost none of its supernatural value. Moreover, whenever she was confronted with a problem or a difficulty, she took refuge in prayer, and more than once, as in the case of Palmerina and Andrea di Naddino de' Bellanti, "the gentle dispute and entreaty lasted the whole night until dawn; finally, mercy conquered justice" (*Leggenda minore*, Part 2, Chap. 7). She knew well that this was her supreme resource, especially when dealing with those in authority, and she often concluded her respectful exhortations with the daring words: "Act in such a way that I shall not have to complain about you to God." This was the method she recommended unreservedly because it is the only means of ensuring that contemplation preserves its radiance and that action remains united to God:

Let your love be like a vessel that you fill at a fountain and by means of which you drink from that fountain. If you withdraw your love from God, who is the fountain of living water, if you do not drink continually of Him, your vessel will be emptied; this will be a proof that you are not drinking fully of God.

(Letter 49, to Monna Alessa.)

Part 3. *The Apostolic Life*

❖❖❖❖❖❖❖❖❖

12. The Cell of Self-Knowledge

❖❖❖❖❖❖❖❖❖

TIME and time again Catherine returns to the absolute
necessity of beginning the spiritual life by building in
one's soul an interior cell into which one can retire to be alone
with God; and no less often she explains that this cell is
simply self-knowledge in God. The expression is so striking
and the metaphor so eloquent that her formula is assured of
success: it is easy to remember and repeat, and, when repeated, it wins admiration and meets with criticism, both
equally superficial. Do you know of even one "spiritual"
person who has become aware of the riches of this doctrine
and who has used it to live better in Christ?

Along with that, an expression such as "self-knowledge in
God" has such an Augustinian flavor that historians halt in
surprise at it and set about seeking out its origins. Here we are
most interested in finding out what this doctrine actually meant
to Catherine and in examining it closely because of the very
fact that she never tired of returning to it. From the first days
of her retreat into solitude, which was her novitiate in the
school of Christ, she received the revelation upon which her
success and her sanctity were to depend:

"Daughter, do you know who you are and who I am? If you
know these two things, you will be blessed. You are she who is

not; I am He who is. . . . Daughter, think of Me; if you do so, I shall immediately think of you."

(*Life,* Part 1, Chap. 10.)

At the end of her life, God made the same recommendation to her, as we find in the conclusion of the *Dialogue:*

"I have answered you by enlightening you with My truth, by showing you the way to know this truth which you so much desire to know. I therefore have taught you that you can come to the knowledge of the truth by knowing Me and by knowing yourself, in the light of faith."

(*Dialogue,* Chap. 166.)

As Catherine saw it, sinners who wish to set out across the bridge that leads to life fail to do so "because the root of self-love has not been completely removed from their souls" (*Dialogue,* Chap. 49). How, then, can we avoid the conclusion that her teaching about the cell of self-knowledge is the expression of one of her most personal experiences and a basic element of her message?

Perhaps we should point out that a translation of Catherine's phrase closer to our way of thinking would be "the cell that is self-knowledge in God," just as we would say "the Mystical Body that is Holy Church" instead of her "the Mystical Body of Holy Church," and "the image that is the creature" instead of "the image of the creature." In striving to understand her thought and to express it in our own language of spirituality, we must remember that our terminology is more abstract than hers and that we live in an age when the metaphor of the cell has no great appeal for most people. The modern equivalent of her dictum would be some formula such as "Make an interior synthesis capable of inspiring all your actions," or "Have guiding principles that are clear enough to supply you with effective inspiration," or "Live your life on the plane of faith," or "Go forward like children of light," or "Manage your life so that you always live in relation to God," or "Attain a love that is conscious enough to be the light of your life."

The metaphor of the cell brings to mind the idea of a retreat in which the soul can renew its strength after the fatigue of the active life, where it can leave aside visible things to think about those that are invisible, and where it finally finds peace, far from external distractions. The old monks used to dream of "passing from cell to celestial life" and of that "happy solitude that is the sole happiness." For the apostolic Catholic, the cell is the center in which he renews his strength and draws new inspiration and strength for his efforts in the service of his brethren. Hence the advice which Catherine gave in her spiritual testament to him who was nearest and dearest to her, Blessed Raymond:

You will rarely have the joy of being in your monastic cell, but I wish you always to carry around with you the cell of your heart because, as you are well aware, as long as we dwell there, the enemy cannot harm us.

(Letter 373, to Raymond of Capua.)

This was her teaching, designed to initiate others into the wonders that she had tasted during the three years she had spent in her cell in the family house on the Via Fontebranda and thus to fit them to work in establishing the kingdom of God, for hers was an apostolic doctrine. The solitude she had in mind allows the apostle to remain alone with God everywhere and, by keeping him unattached to anyone on earth, to make himself the servant of all and to put himself at God's disposal as an instrument of divine love.

What, then, is this blessed "self-knowledge" that can

bring about such good effects? It is by no means a self-centered, psychological knowledge. Catherine had learned that God thinks of those who think of Him and she would seek self-knowledge only to help her in transforming herself into Christ. Even less is it an egoistical contemplation of self, nor is it self-complacency. To her mind, self-knowledge should result in a closer and more sincere clinging to God. The soul must not be like Narcissus, who forgot everything but his own reflection to the extent that he wasted away and was reduced to nothing more than a flickering image in the water. To Catherine, the reflection causes us to love the fountain in which we are reflected:

[The soul] looks at itself in the spring that issues from the ocean of the Divine Essence. Its desire disposes it to love itself in God and to love God in itself, like a person who, contemplating his own image in the water of a fountain, is pleased with himself and rejoices in himself. But if he is wise, he will love, more than himself, the fountain which permits him to see and love himself, and which, by showing him the defects in his countenance, allows him to correct them.

(Letter 226, to Raymond of Capua.)

From this it is plain to see the source from which self-knowledge is drawn: we achieve it, not by self-analysis or introspection, but by cleaving to God. "The soul does not see itself by looking at itself but by looking at God, and it sees God by looking at Him as the Sovereign Good, worthy of our love" (Ibid.). It is from God that the soul learns what it is, and that is why, in discovering itself, it learns to love God: "Contemplating in itself the effect of infinite love, and seeing the image that is the creature, it finds God in His image" (Ibid.). The Dialogue insistently shows that we must not separate self-knowledge from knowledge of God, a point which Catherine never tired of stressing in her letters, too:

I strongly wish you to see your nothingness, your negligence and your ignorance; but I want you to see them, not in the darkness of confusion, but in the light of the divine goodness that you find within you. Learn that the demon only wants you to stop at the mere knowledge of your defects, whereas this knowledge should always be accompanied by the hope of obtaining God's mercy.

(Letter 73, to Sister Costanza.)

Far from being a "natural" method or simply a kind of edifying practice, this self-appraisal is so supernatural and so centered upon God that it is to be sought in Christ, who is God made like to us. Continuing her metaphor, Catherine pictures it as the stone curb surrounding the fountain:

Let us give glory to God and service to our neighbor without ever becoming separated from the object of our love, which is Jesus crucified. He is the wall upon which you must lean in order to see yourself in the fountain. Run, run to Him. Hide yourself in the wounds of Jesus crucified.

(Letter 226, to Raymond of Capua.)

When we view it in this light, we can easily understand the nature of self-knowledge as Catherine saw it:

Open the eye of your mind, give ear and listen to His doctrine. Look at yourself because you will find yourself in Him and you will find Him in you. You will find yourself in Him because He has created you in His own image and likeness out of His freely bestowed love. You will find in yourself this measureless goodness of God which has made Him take on our likeness by uniting His divine nature with our human nature. May our hearts melt and be filled to overflowing with the contemplation of this marvel of burning love—God grafted on to man and man on to God. O ineffable love! If men could only appreciate it, that alone would be enough!

(Ibid.)

In other words, self-knowledge shows us our relationship to God and the love that brought that relationship about, first in the order of nature and creation, and then in the order of grace and redemption, in which the Christian sees that God loved him to the point of seeking him out by undergoing the humiliations of the redeeming Incarnation and by making him a member of His Mystical Body. Catherine returns again and again to these two themes, and it is indeed worth our while to examine her thoughts on them more closely because thereby we shall learn the exact nature of the self-knowledge which she regarded as a condition for apostolic sanctity. Sometimes she lays greatest stress upon man's original wretchedness but, even then, she cannot stop at that wretchedness but goes on to make use of it in reaching a better insight into God's love:

Neither riches nor rank nor worldly honor brings us to this degree of real and genuine virtue. Nor does it mean being exalted in dignity or being presumptuous. No, it is solely the knowledge that the soul has of itself. Thanks to this knowledge, the soul sees that it does not exist of itself but by the power of God. It knows its wretchedness and weakness, the time that it has obviously lost and during which it could have made precious gains. In this light, it sees both its own baseness and its own dignity. It sees its baseness in the coarse envelope of its body, which is the food of death, the food of worms, and nothing but a bag of filth; and yet we take more pleasure in loving and satisfying this putrid bag and in pandering to it, at the urging of sensual love, than in the riches of the soul, whose dignity is, nevertheless, so great that it could not be greater. For we see that God, urged by His burning love, has willed to create us, not in the state of unthinking animals, nor like the angels, but in His own image and likeness. To fulfill His dignity in us, that is to say, with a view to procuring for us the end for which He has created us, and to perfect our dignity, He Himself took on our image when He clothed His divinity with our humanity. He gave us back grace, creating us anew in the blood of the sweet and all-loving Word, His only-begotten Son, who has redeemed us, not with silver, but with blood. Moreover, the value of the blood which He has paid for us, and God's union with men, show us the ineffable love that God has accorded us and the dignity which we received at the first creation, as we have been told.

(Letter 334, to Cardinal Bonaventura of Padua.)

Yet, no matter how exalted this knowledge may be, Catherine's intention was too realistic and her love too genuine to prevent her from searching for a light that could aid her in her interior efforts: "We shall not know our dignity and the defects that corrupt the beauty of our soul unless we plunge our gaze in the ocean of peace that is the divine essence, in which we shall find ourselves again" (Letter 226, to Raymond of Capua). This luminous clarity of vision was all the more necessary because she looked upon asceticism as a battle —we could say a hand-to-hand battle—in which each virtue is developed only by struggling against and overcoming the contrary temptation: "As you see, when we are in darkness it is not the time to flee or complain, because light is born of darkness. O God, sweet love! How sweet is Your teaching! Virtue is acquired through that which is contrary to it!" And, when she had established this principle by applying it to purity, humility and patience, she continued: "Reflect on this: the soul can neither receive nor desire virtue if it does not want to bear persecutions and temptations with true, holy patience for love of Jesus crucified" (Letter 211, to Raymond of Capua).

She then goes on:

Do not lose time. Strive to know yourself so that this queen [patience] may be the guest of your soul. Her presence is very necessary to you.

It is the means whereby we ascend the cross with Jesus crucified and there share His food. . . . The soul thus lives in the cell of knowledge of God's goodness, in itself. There it grows fat [that is, healthy and vigorous].

Note the words "the cell of knowledge of God's goodness, in itself," which show the nature and spirit of this knowledge, just as the effects of this knowledge show its concrete, vivifying character: it is knowledge that "fattens," that is, strengthens and gives joy.

In this way, to use the words of a newer and more profound formula, the soul will succeed in "espousing the truth," just as St. Francis of Assisi espoused Lady Poverty. The soul becomes one of "the children of light," as the Gospel says:

In fact, it is this light that gives fidelity to the soul, freeing it from the deceptions of sensuality, and, when it is dead to its natural tastes, making it run in the footsteps of Christ crucified, who is Truth itself. Because of this light, the heart becomes serious, firm and unshakeable and does not allow itself to be led into impatience by trials or into inordinate joy by success and consolation; instead it retains the proper balance on every occasion. He who is enlightened by this light always acts prudently and is happier listening to necessary discourses than giving useless ones, because he has seen in this light that what God loves is few words and many works.

(Letter 330, to Raymond of Capua.)

This knowledge is never a turning back upon self because, by showing us the love with which God loves our brethren as much as us, it becomes a motive for charity. As Catherine points out:

When the soul contemplates in itself the effect of infinite love, and sees the image that is the creature, it finds God in His image. It sees

118

that the love which God has for it extends to every creature, and this impels it immediately to love the neighbor as itself because God loves him sovereignly.

(Letter 226, to Raymond of Capua.)

That is why this knowledge becomes a principle of the apostolic life and of the desire that is its inspiration and measure:

In its own cell, [the soul] painfully eats souls as its food—as its food because its table is the cross. In the cell of the praise and glory of God, it makes its bed of repose. Therefore it has its table and its food, it has the Holy Spirit as servant, and it has as its bed of repose the Eternal Father's glory. Happy to have found such a sweet cell within itself, it defends it from the outside world with all its strength.

(Letter 104, to Raymond of Capua.)

This cell does not restrict or close the soul up in itself but is rather a hearth from which warmth radiates to the outside world, a sharing which does not make the soul "exterior" but which, instead, unites it to God and to everything that has to do with Him: in a word, the cell inspires "desire."

As Catherine saw it, self-knowledge in God—or, better, the knowledge of God in oneself—must become a permanent state; it must be the light that illuminates the whole of life. She does insist on the soul's duty to retire to this retreat in order to regain its balance, as St. Peter retired to weep over his denial of Christ, but the very word cell clearly means a permanent dwelling place, a retreat in which one can set up house. It is not simply "wood thrown on the fire" to cause a blaze, but is the essential element in the soul's habitual outlook. That is why it would perhaps be better to express Catherine's doctrine in the language of the Gospel, using St. John's own words, "[to stand] in the truth" (see John 8:44), so as to avoid a metaphor that runs the risk of attenuating her thought.

We must therefore act in such a way that the mind will constantly consider and recognize its own nothingness and the goodness of God in us, for He is who is. That is the way in which continual prayer is gradually perfected, because continual prayer is nothing else than a holy desire and a sweet movement of love, and love follows the mind.

(Letter 22, to Abbot Martino de Passignano.)

The apostolate, then, will be this desire translated into deeds.

This self-knowledge—in which self is dissolved in the love of God and the neighbor—does not turn the contemplative in upon himself but rather transforms him, making him a true apostle in the spirit of St. Paul, a phrase that is rich in significance, implying that he must be a man of desires, thinking only of God's glory and devoting himself thereto. Thus, the rule of the apostolic spirit will not apply solely to a task such as devoting oneself exclusively to a particular duty or to the correct performance of a particular function. To desire means to go out of oneself and to take as one's term of reference something outside oneself.

In Catherine's doctrine, desire shows emphatically that the inspiration which produces prayer and which should regulate our actions is not the search for an opportunity to give ourselves or to give of ourselves in some activity sought out in accordance with our own tastes or ideas; nor is it the resolve to confine ourselves to the accomplishment of the duties of our state, as if these duties were to be considered sufficient in themselves. Rather, it is a veritable torment that is inspired by the desire to imitate the love of God wishing to give Himself to men. It is a striving to share in Christ's thirst to draw everything to Him. Our desires will not be limited to the confines of human ability, because prayer opens to us a world in which the standard is, not our weakness, but rather God's merciful intention to give Himself to the world.

Our insight into God's love is perfected by our consciousness of our nothingness and sin, and it is thus that we shall obtain the strength to persevere. We must mention here Catherine's beautiful letter to Pietro, son of Giovanni Venturi (Letter 47), in which she demonstrates the necessity of self-knowledge for truly living out the mystery of divine love.

13. Humility

CATHERINE very often identifies self-knowledge with humility—which is not surprising, since it is only logical that we should live according to the light we receive from God. Still, if we are to follow her thought as closely as possible, we shall find it instructive to consider humility as the fruit of self-knowledge: "Humility springs from self-knowledge as the clear stream flows from the well-spring" (Letter 49, to Monna Alessa).

The trials through which the Saint passed demonstrate how solid was her humility, for neither petty annoyances nor savage hatred were able to shake it. When people cannot understand someone or something, they often revenge themselves by mockery, disparagement and calumny. As a result, Catherine was subjected to every kind of humiliation, but she never lost courage when she was abused and calumniated by the sick people she nursed so devotedly, when she met with the undisguised hostility of cardinals blinded by the luxury of life in Avignon, or when she was exposed to the mockery of her fellow townsmen and to the violence of the mobs in Florence and Rome which not only cried out for her death but actually tried to kill her. Without pausing to examine each of these incidents in detail (which would take a whole book), we should like to be able to read her mind and know how she felt when she received her extraordinary graces, achieved her heroic victories and worked diligently at her prodigious mission. What were her innermost thoughts? As a matter of fact, she herself tells us. We even have a record of the words she addressed to God on the threshold of eternity, at the moment when, faced with the last reckoning, souls are proverbially most sincere. The passage is rather lengthy, yet it is well worth quoting because it shows both her humility and the main concerns of her spiritual life:

"It is my fault, O Eternal Trinity! I have offended You so miserably by my numerous negligences, my blindness, ingratitude, disobedience and many other defects! Wretch that I am, I have not kept either Your commandments, which bind everyone in general, or those which Your goodness laid on me in particular, on me, a miserable wretch!" And she struck her breast hard, repeating: "Through my fault! Through my fault!" Then she continued: "I have not kept the commandment You gave me to seek to give You glory always and in everything, and to spend myself unceasingly for my neighbor! I have fled from work and sometimes even from duty. O Eternal God, You asked me to abandon myself to You in everything so as to seek only Your glory and the praise of Your name in the salvation of souls. I ought to have taken delight in partaking of this food at the table of the most holy cross, and instead I have sought consolation for myself! You have always invited me to do violence to You by ardent desires, by the sweetest supplications of love, by tears, by humble and continuous prayers for the salvation of the whole world and the reform of Holy Church! You have promised me in return that, by these means, You will show mercy to the world and will reform your Spouse! And I, an unhappy wretch, have not responded to Your advances but have remained asleep on the bed of my negligence! Miserable wretch that I am, You placed me in charge of guiding souls, You gave me all those dear sons so that I might love them with special love, so that my solicitude might lead them to You along the road of truth, and I have been a mirror of iniquity to them! I have not had the zeal I should have had for them, and I have not helped them by humble, continual prayer poured out before You! I have not given them the example of a good, holy life, so as to reinforce what I taught them by word!

"Alas, wretch that I am, I have not received with due veneration the innumerable gifts, the graces of those very numerous and very sweet torments caused by those pains which You were pleased to heap upon this frail body of mine, nor have I borne them with that ardent desire, that fiery love that made You bestow them upon me!

"Alas, my love, in Your goodness You chose me as Your spouse from the days of my childhood, and I have not been faithful! I have failed You! I have not been able to keep my memory filled only with You and Your immense benefactions. I have not kept my mind fixed on Your will and devoted only to seeking Your good pleasure; nor did I use my will to love You with all my strength and without reserve, as You asked me to do."

(Catherine's last prayers on her deathbed,
Fioretti, pp. 183–185.)

This is truly attractive humility. Catherine was not a woman who counted grains of dust and was afraid of her own shadow but, rather, a great soul who saw and accepted the truth. After all her accomplishments, she saw herself as nothingness in the presence of Being itself, non-love as compared with Love itself, and impotence as compared with Strength itself. Such humility is in no danger of being frightened off or compromised by compliments or successes of any kind. Basically, the chasm between "Him who is and her who is not" remains infinite, as she was acutely aware:

"May thanks upon thanks be given You, O Eternal Father! You

have not disdained me, the work of Your hands; You have not turned Your face from me; You have not scorned my desires. O Light, You have not held me to account for my darkness! O Life, You have not been disheartened by me, who am death! O Divine Physician, You have never turned away from my greatly ailing body! O Eternal Purity, You have bent down to the dunghill of my defects! You, who are infinite, have leaned down to me, who am finite; You, who are Wisdom, to me, who am foolish. Despite the infinite evil and defects that are in me, Your wisdom, bounty, clemency and infinite goodness have never despised me."

(*Dialogue*, Chap. 167.)

This is not the humility of a pure contemplative seeing himself as he stands alone before God's face, but rather that of an apostle assessing himself in relation to his responsibilities, which are immense. "I confess, O infinite God, O mysterious and eternal Deity, I confess and do not deny that I, a miserable wretch, am the cause of all evil because I did not use the light in Your light" (Prayer 18).

Whence came this humility of Catherine's which triumphs did not puff up nor trials depress? It certainly did not arise from the mere consideration of her wretchedness and faults. Rather, she learned it more from the cross, which held her spellbound, than from her own reasoning and experience. She estimated the immensity of her misery from the greatness of the remedy it demanded. This is more than a thirst for truth: it is the reaching out of an impassioned love that is intoxicated with the desire to become lowly so as to be nearer the Beloved.

One evening, when she had spent a day filled with fatigue and annoyances, our Lord appeared to her with two crowns, one of gold and the other of thorns, and eagerly she grasped the crown of pain and ignominy. She therefore had a right to give this advice:

Love God, serve Him with all your heart, with all your strength, without reserve and with true, profound humility, loving your neighbor as yourself. You will say to me: How can I have this humility? I shall answer that, if you will, you can, with the grace of God, who never refuses it to him who asks for it. The real way [to obtain humility] is to contemplate God's humility and charity in the [divine] light. His humility is so profound that men's minds are confounded by it. Has the like ever been seen in a creature? Of course not. And is there anything more astonishing than to see God humbled to man's level, and the sovereign might of the Deity brought down to such abasement?

God has clothed Himself in our humanity; He has visibly conversed with men; He has borne our infirmities and poverty and wretchedness; He has humbled Himself even to the shameful death on the cross. His sovereign might has become small in order to confound the proud, who always seek to exalt themselves and who do not perceive that they are falling into deep wretchedness. You will find in Him the source of the humility that makes Him visit the soul of every rational creature. . . . It is through the knowledge of God's goodness and the light that makes us see His humility and charity that we acquire this virtue, searching for it in the depths of our souls. Otherwise we shall never possess it.

(Letter 345, to Contessa Giovanna.)

We can believe her when she extols the advantages of humility, one of which seemed to her to sum up all the others and to express what we can call the spiritual function of humility: "It is the nurse of charity." When we are confronted with our neighbor, our awareness of his misery and of God's goodness will make us humble and merciful, completely devoted to him and ready to serve him even to the extent of washing his feet.

Humility, which leads us to self-knowledge in God, has a twin sister, confidence. We know that we can do nothing without God, but we also know that we can do everything with Him, and this gives us a sense of security. When we consider the peace that reigned in Catherine's soul, we can easily see the reason for her confidence. As she herself so pointedly remarked: "Those who hope only in themselves are afraid of their own shadow and fear that heaven and earth are going to let them down" (*Dialogue*, Chap. 119). Her whole life, which seemed to defy all the laws of nature and the laws of custom and the social order (which are perhaps even more unchangeable still), was founded on confidence in God. Her missions as ambassador, her journeys to Avignon, and her work to repair the schism were the daring, even the seemingly foolhardy, result of her confidence in God and her magnanimity.

The three virtues of humility, confidence and magnanimity are, in the loving soul, the daughters of truth. To Monna Alessa, Catherine wrote:

Make yourself the least of all, subject to every creature in humility and patience, not excusing yourself, but saying *Mea culpa*. And thus, by the virtue of humility, you will overcome vice in your own soul and in the souls of those to whom you teach this lesson.

(Letter 49.)

In another letter to the same friend, she unburdened herself much more freely than was her custom, confiding that she felt as if she were "on an island beaten by winds from every direction." Here also she summed up her whole life by remarking that the Lord

takes account of holy desires and not of creatures. He has not removed from me His bounty despite my ingratitude, despite my meager light and intelligence, but has taken account only of Himself, who is sovereignly good.

(Letter 119.)

127

14. The Sword of Hate

WHEN we scrutinize ourselves in the revealing light of Sovereign Truth, we shall first of all discover that we have in us the seeds of death—the flesh lusting against the spirit, overweening self-confidence, the desire to seek our own ease, the urge to be seen by others and to dominate them, and all the most shameful sins. It is no wonder that St. Catherine, viewing such disorder, sighed with compassion: "Behold the work of self-love, the source of pride and of every vice!"

What, then, are we to do? Confronted as we are with evidence so clear, we do not need to spend much time in seeking the remedy:

Give God the things that are God's and give the earth the things that belong to it. We must give God our hearts, souls and love, quickly and without negligence. All your actions should be founded on God. What shall we give to the earth, that is to say, to our sensual natures? The thing it deserves! And what does something that kills deserve? It deserves to die!

(Letter 21, to an unnamed person.)

This was certainly clear enough; yet, to make sure that her

disciples understood what she meant, Catherine did not spare them. She put it bluntly: "Dearest children, I desire that, even while you live in this life, you strive to be dead to all self-will, for it is with that death that you will acquire virtue" (Letter 192, to Neri di Landoccio), meaning that we must renounce our earthly appetites, desires and pleasures. She wished to reduce the sensual element in man to a state of "death that neither sees nor hears nor feels" (Letter 344, to Raymond of Capua). But she also observed that it is not a question of killing the life of the senses but rather of extinguishing and removing the fire of corruption. Nothing is to be spared, neither so-called "spiritual" self-love nor the desire to seek one's own satisfaction and vanity in God: "To the extent that the vessel of the heart is full of spiritual or temporal self-love, it cannot be filled with divine love" (Letter 80, to Maestro Giovanni Tantucci).

Are we, then, to try to reach a compromise, a reconciliation between self-love and love of God? Catherine answered: "Since it is impossible to live without love, and since two contrary loves cannot exist together, the soul must strip itself of sinful love and clothe itself with the love of God" (Letter 287, to Fra Niccolò di Nanni). She wanted to keep her disciples in a continual state of war on self: "I wish each of you to separate in himself sensuality and reason, and to make them irreconcilable enemies" (Letter 332, to Pietro di Giovanni and Stefano Maconi).

By paying the price of death to self, the soul finds peace and true life. Catherine used to say that "nothing ensures the security and strength of a soul as much as this holy hatred" (*Life*, Part 1, Chap. 10). In addition, the soul then tastes peace and tranquility of spirit:

It has found peace in war because it has rooted out self-will based

129

on pride and has conceived divine grace in its spirit. It carries Christ crucified in the depth of its spirit and seeks to know nothing but Christ crucified. There it smothers its own will and becomes humble and obedient.

(Letter 38, to Monna Agnesa.)

There the soul finds also that strength and manliness which so surprise and captivate us in Catherine, who fortunately shares her secret with us: "We shall be manly because that feminine desire to please which makes the heart cowardly will be extinguished in us."

The means to be used to attain this victory and this happy state is the "dagger" or "sword of hatred," terms which well express the energetic and uncompromising nature of the method to be used. The Saint defined the sword of hatred in these words:

The more a soul possesses the love of God, the more holy hatred it has for the sensory part [of man], for its own sensuality, because the love of God naturally begets hatred for faults committed against God. For the soul sees that concupiscence, the origin and source of every fault, reigns within, and plunges its roots into, the sensory part. Then it feels itself seized with a great hatred, a holy hatred, for this life of the senses, and it exerts every effort, not to kill this life, but to pluck out the source of corruption that is rooted in it. That cannot be done without a long, total war on sensuality itself. Furthermore, it is not possible that there should not remain some roots capable of producing at least light faults, which is a new motive for the soul to be displeased with itself. . . . Nothing ensures the security and strength of a soul as much as this holy hatred.

(Leggenda minore, Part 1, Chap. 10.)

Catherine's views were not solely the result of her temperament. No doubt she was, by nature, averse to half measures, as was apparent from her penances, which, although they were the effects of a miracle, were none the less the fruit of virtue and the result of personal effort. For example, she confessed that nothing cost her so much as conquering the desire for sleep. Rather, her teaching is part of that fiery intransigence which, when she was fifteen, made her cut off her hair, which later made her drink pus because she was indignant at herself for being disgusted by a creature redeemed by Christ, and which, all her life, made her accept injuries and trials with a joyous heart. Her method has an element more universal than a particular type of temperament; it aims at unmasking the perfidy of sensuality, which finds support and aid in the world around us:

Let reason arm itself with the sword of hate and love. This war must not be a lifeless, but rather a vigorous, enterprise. Sensuality absolutely must be killed because it robs us of the life of grace by making us resist God. This accursed law [of sensuality] sometimes employs a subtle trick to make us fall more dangerously. It sleeps and seems dead in us: we do not feel any inner struggle; on the contrary, we are full of fervor, and all our actions, all our thoughts, are directed to God with a sweetness that seems like a foretaste of eternal life. But if we relax our warfare, if we lay down the sword and are lacking in vigilance, it arises within us more strongly than ever and causes us to fall grievously. . . . Courage, therefore, my children! Take up this sword and let it never leave the hands of your free will until you die.
(Letter 332, to Pietro di Giovanni and Stefano Maconi.)

This energy is the condition for virtue: "The virtues are acquired painfully, by doing violence to our weakness" (Letter 318, to Sano di Maco and others). "It's by holy striving, by conquering our perverse wills, and by violence that we shall acquire true, solid virtues, and our pains will be rewarded with immortal goods" (Letter 48, to Matteo, son of Giovanni

131

Colombini of Siena). Union with God is acquired only at this price: "We lack God to the same extent that we retain part of ourselves" (Letter 98, to Fra Tommaso della Fonte).

> "[The soul] goes on, carrying the cup of its heart, finally emptied of all self-will and inordinate love; but as soon as it is emptied, it is refilled, for nothing can remain empty. Once it is emptied of perishable things, the air fills it—that is to say, the sweet, heavenly divine love whereby the soul arrives at the water of grace. As soon as it reaches that point, it passes through the door, which is Christ crucified, and tastes the living water as it finds itself in Me, who am the ocean of peace."
>
> (*Dialogue*, Chap. 54.)

Christ's jealous love and the demands of His Blood make us His property because, "once bought back [by Him], we cannot sell ourselves again" (Letter 24, to Biringhieri degli Arzocchi). Catherine wrote to her niece Sister Eugenia,

So that that may not happen, be careful never to have the misfortune of having a special affection for a man, religious or secular. If I could know it or find it out, even though I were farther away than I am now, I would give you such a penance that you would remember it all your life, whether you liked to or not. . . . Be careful that you do not bind your heart to anyone but Jesus crucified; otherwise, when you would wish to free it, you would not be able to do so, which would be very difficult for you. I have told you that the soul which satisfies itself with the food of angels has seen in the [divine] light that these things are obstacles to this food, and it flees them most zealously.

(Letter 26.)

I want no one but God to be present in your heart. Remove all self-love, all sensory affection for your relatives or for anything else; and do so without any fear of life or death, but with a heart free and clothed in this holy garment [obedience]. Place yourself in the hands

132

of your heavenly Spouse, abandon yourself to His will so that He may do or undo as is best for His glory and for you.

(Letter 54, to a nun in the Convent of St. Agnes of Montepulciano.)

Remember that your Spouse, Christ, sweet Jesus, wishes that there be no obstacle between you and Him. He is very jealous, and as soon as He sees that you love something else besides Him, He will withdraw from you and you will be worthy to eat only the food of beasts. (Letter 26.)

Finally, the needs of the Church require this manliness:

Cast far from you all tenderness toward yourself and all servile fear, because the Church does not need such people but rather those who are cruel to themselves and compassionate to her.

(Letter 373, to Raymond of Capua.)

These reasons and many similar ones are found in the advice she gave to her disciples "to kick the world away" and to "cut through entanglements rather than lose time in untying them." A letter to her dear son, Stefano Maconi, is worth quoting in its entirety:

Dearest son in sweet Christ Jesus, I, Catherine, the servant and slave of the servants of Jesus Christ, am writing to you in His precious Blood with the desire to see you possessed of sufficient light and knowledge to understand that you must cut away and not untie, because he who does not cut away remains forever bound, and he who does not flee remains a prisoner. No longer resist the Holy Spirit, who is calling you. Resistance will be hard for you. Do not allow yourself to be trammelled by a tepid heart, by a love that is womanish and pitiful, and that often has the appearance of virtue. But rather be manly; take to the battlefield like a man, keeping before your mind's eye the Blood shed with such fiery love so that, once

133

freed, you may be spurred on to combat. Answer, answer, my careless son! Open the door of your heart! It is a great insult that God should be at the door of your soul and that it should not be opened to Him. Do not be mercenary with Him but, rather, faithful to Him. Bathe in the Blood of Christ crucified. There you will find the knife of hatred and love; you will cut away every bond alien to God's will and every obstacle to perfection, and you will find the light you need to see that you must cut. I shall say no more to you about it. Live in the sweet, holy love of God. Sweet Jesus, Jesus love!

(Letter 205.)

We must not think that the sword of hate is to be used haphazardly. On the contrary, the Saint wished the strokes of the sword to be aimed accurately, with the intent to slay a specific enemy:

Therefore, my beloved children, I want you in all things to apply yourselves to killing that perverse sensuous will which ceaselessly wishes to rebel against God. Here is the way to go about it. Take your place upon the exalted seat of your conscience in order to judge yourself. Do not allow even the smallest thought outside of God to pass without correcting it very severely. Man must divide himself into two parts, sensuality and reason. Reason must draw from its scabbard the sword with two edges, hatred of vice and love of virute. Armed with this sword, reason will make sensuality surrender unconditionally.

(Letter 255, to Francesco di Pipino, a tailor in Florence.)

Elsewhere she advises:

Visit the garden of your soul every day in the light of faith, to pluck out the thorns that would choke the good seed, and to turn over the soil, that is to say, to strip your heart. This stripping is absolutely necessary. Very often I have seen those who seem to be stripped [of self] and I have found them clothed when I paid more attention

134

to their deeds than to their words. Words often deceive, but actions show the, reality.

(Letter 119, to Monna Alessa.)

She repeats this same advice in writing to the indiscreet Sister Daniella:

It is by hating yourself, by increasing the reproaches which you heap upon yourself, by considering who He is whom you offend and who you are who offend Him, by remembering death and by loving virtue that you will succeed in killing vice in your soul and in tearing out its roots. Penance only cuts [the weeds] but in this way you pluck out the root that is always ready to produce a new shoot.

(Letter 213.)

It is plain then that Catherine meant exactly what she said, that she wants to lead us to death—violent, all-embracing death. She is the faithful echo of our Lord's command to take up the cross and follow Him. However, this path of death leads us to true life:

"The path of penance and of My commandments at first appears rugged and difficult, but the more one advances on it, the sweeter and easier it becomes. The path of vice, on the contrary, at first seems very pleasant, but the more one walks along it, the more bitterness and ruins one finds."

(*Life*, Part 1, Chap. 9.)

This is so because, basically, hatred of self is simply the other side of the coin of love for Christ. When Catherine prayed, "Lord, I beg You to teach me the virtue with which You most love to enrich Your servants," the Lord replied, "Above all else, I ask My servants to hate themselves and to love Me perfectly" (Caffarini, *Supplemento*, Part 2, Chap. 3). She found in the Blood of Christ the strength and desire for this love and this hate. Accordingly, she earnestly counselled one of her dearest disciples: "Drown yourself in the Blood of Christ crucified, where everything bitter becomes sweet, and every heavy burden light" (Letter 169, to Fra Matteo dei Tolomei and Dom Niccolò di Francia).

15. Holy Discretion

❖❖❖❖❖❖❖❖❖

THE war against self-love must be carefully directed: our whole life and all our activities must be so guided that we do not deviate from our purpose; or, to use another metaphor, we must never leave the helm. This is especially true for those of us who live "in the world," where change and unforeseen circumstances so often occur, where there is neither rule nor superior to guide us, where "men are placed in the hands of their own counsel." Herein lies the role of the virtue of prudence, refined and made more spiritual by the gifts of knowledge and counsel. Theologians see this high degree of prudence in St. Catherine's "holy discretion," which was such a marked characteristic of her life and teaching as well as of her mode of action when she came in contact with "the world."

There is no need to emphasize that this prudence has nothing in common with that false prudence whose motto is "Don't rock the boat!" and which worldly people recommend; and it has still less to do with the prudence of the fox in the fable. This real prudence can sometimes be abstention from, or deliberation in, action or it can be "enlightened opportunism." It means having a sense of one's responsibilities and a consciousness of one's rights; and it is no less prudence when it becomes "the folly of the cross." It is the virtue that enables us properly to take the initiative and assume responsibility. Therefore, those souls that lack boldness because they do not possess true judgment can profit from learning that Catherine was being prudent when she exposed herself to leprosy, when she fasted or imposed harsh penances on herself in trying to meet the needs of her neighbor, or when she risked her reputation to save a soul; and they will also see that she was being prudent when she urged the Pope to return to Rome, as well as when she negotiated important affairs.

The striking combination of audacity and confidence, respect and frankness, obedience and zeal, which is so evident in Catherine's mode of action, reveals a high degree of prudence. It was this characteristic that especially impressed Raymond of Capua, the spiritual director who knew her best and whose testimony has particular weight because he himself was eminently a prudent man. While he was still quite young, he had been given confidential missions in the Order, and later he exercised the highest functions in the government of his brethren. In addition, the Sovereign Pontiffs entrusted him with many delicate tasks.

Catherine was prudent in her words and advice, knowing how to adapt herself to the needs and circumstances of each individual. She was prudent in her almsgiving, being able to distinguish between those who were in real need and those who were not. It is the function of prudence to help us to choose appropriate means toward the end we wish to attain, to show us exactly where we stand, and to enable us to see the possibilities and the disadvantages in a particular line of action. Catherine learned this discretion from God and made it a central element in her doctrine. Basically, holy discretion, which is composed of light and strength, makes us respond to the demands of divine love, demands which are as personal and incommunicable as love and which, like love, are always total demands.

What are the constituent elements of holy discretion? First, there is reason and all its resources. Catherine, a great mystic, did not agree with those who despise reason; on the contrary, she esteemed it: "Would it not be a very shameful thing if we, who are rational creatures, did not use our reason any more than the animals?" (Letter 13, to Marco Bindi).

Holy discretion is also composed of the light of faith, which teaches us the infinite resources and the increasing demands of grace: "What, in fact, is discretion but the true knowledge that the soul should have of itself and of Me? Its root, therefore, is sunk deep in this knowledge" (*Dialogue*, Chap. 9). Discretion presupposes, too, the love of God and the neighbor, a love whose aim dictates the means to be used: "It is a shoot grafted on and united to charity" (*Jbid.*) In addition, discretion contains all the enlightenment that God gives the soul.

The role of supernatural discernment is first and above all to show the infinite distance between the end and the means. Both in the *Dialogue* and in her letter to Sister Daniella, St. Catherine puts this function in first place. The whole spiritual life would be compromised if the end and the means were confused with each other. God wants infinite works, and the soul must expand to meet His demands. He wants few words and many actions or, rather, He wishes to see above all else our love in our works. Holy discretion, then, establishes harmony among the means, and guides them to the single goal—love: "The soul cannot be set up on two foundations: one or the other must be thrown to the ground. And that which is not the principal one must become an instrument" (Letter 213, to Sister Daniella). Further on, Catherine remarks: "Do not seek to let the lesser good, penance, impede the greater" (*Ibid.*). Then, deeming it appropriate that she should prove her point from her own experience, she continues: "I have found many penitents who lack patience and obedience because they have applied themselves to killing their bodies but not their wills. That is what comes of following the rule of indiscretion."

Prudence supplies a rule for soul and body, for thoughts and deeds—the rule of love, for, while this love is one in essence, it is universal in its applications, which are achieved by prudence. Holy discretion learns to love God without measure, to give Him everything just as it has received everything from Him.

In regard to the neighbor, it reminds us of the inestimable value of charity, causing us to be more intent on supplying our neighbor's bodily needs than on piling up riches for ourselves, to think more of his soul than of the needs of his body and to esteem God more than men's souls. As Catherine said:

You should speak moderately even with those whom you love with a spiritual love. If you do not do so, remember that the measureless love which you should have for God will suffer thereby because finite creatures will be an obstacle to that love. . . . You will love it [the creature] with the measureless love which you owe to God, and this will be an obstacle to your perfection because you should love even spiritually with due measure.

(Letter 49, to Monna Alessa.)

And her sense of God's sovereignty made her reject the false reasons that are given for going against God's laws:

Inordinate love sometimes makes us commit faults by living according to the senses or trying to please our neighbor. This should never be, because well-regulated love in God never wishes to sacrifice the soul, even to save the whole world. Even if by committing one sin it were possible to ensure eternal life for every rational creature, then that sin must not be committed.

(Letter 254, to Pietro, son of Jacomo Attacusi de' Tolomei of Siena.)

Finally, discretion must inspire us to act with holy audacity and to reject the timidity and hesitation dictated by carnal prudence. When Raymond refused to allow Catherine and one of her women friends to go to the court of Queen Giovanna of Naples because he feared for "the virgins' reputation," she answered him boldly:

If [Saints] Agnes and Margaret had thought as you do, they would never have won the crown of martyrdom. Have we not a Spouse who can snatch us from the hands of the ungodly and preserve our purity even amidst a mob of depraved men? Your fears are vain and come from too weak a faith rather than from real prudence.

(*Life*, Part 3, Chap. 1.)

The prudence of true love of God knows its own weakness as well as it knows the resources of infinite mercy, which are even closer at hand.

16. The Will of God

❖❖❖❖❖❖❖❖❖

"ONLY those who do God's will are united to Him by love" (Letter 215, to some convents in Bologna). All the aspirations of our love, all our efforts reach their goal and all the complexities of life are unified in the one center, the will of God. Even eternal life, as Catherine said, "is nothing other than a will at peace, in harmony with the will of God, a docile will which can desire and will only what God wills; and the whole happiness of those who rejoice in it is founded upon this pacified will" (Letter 5, to Messer Francesco da Montalcino). *La dolce mamma* also bequeathed to her disciples this obedience to God's will as a companion for every moment, as a joy and a spouse: "The obedience which our holy *mamma* gave me as a spouse . . ." (Letter of Stefano Maconi to Neri di Landoccio, quoted in the supplement to the *Leggenda minore*, p. 299 and p. 367, note 73).

Here again, Catherine's virtues and the graces she received inspired and confirmed her teaching. One such grace, less well-known than the exchange of hearts and less extraordinary in form but no less precious and real, was the conformity of her will with, and, as it were, the absorption of her will into, the will of God. Our human words are crude instruments indeed when it comes to describing her state of soul.

142

She saw and heard things so sublime that our corruptible tongues cannot express them. Their beauty and sweetness were such that she asserted that the spiritual or temporal consolations of this life were nothing in comparison. Yet she ardently desired to be deprived of them so as to be more acceptable in God's presence. That same day, when she had prayed Jesus to remove completely all of her own will and to give her His, the Lord replied: "Behold, My well-beloved daughter, I clothe you in My will, in which you shall be so founded and strengthened that, from now on, you shall remain intent on Me without agitation or emotion in everything that shall happen to you."

(*Leggenda minore*, Part 2, Chap. 6.)

And, in fact, her well-loved son was able to say that "she found God in everything through a love that was warm and living" (*Ibid.*, Prologue). The transformation of her will was so obvious and so perfect that she saw nothing strange in remarking "Thus you will do God's will and mine." Despite her humility, truth compelled her to say that she had never failed in obedience (see *Leggenda minore*, Part 1, Chap. 9). Her reactions on various occasions are very revealing in this regard. For example, when an evil spirit threatened to possess her, she simply replied: "If that is the Lord's will, without whose permission I know you can do nothing, I shall be very careful not to put any obstacle in the way and not to assent to the least disagreement with that holy will" (*Life*, Part 2, Chap.

In God's will she found infinite Wisdom and Love adapting itself to us, ruling our lives and leading us to sanctity in time and eternity. God had said to her: "If My Providence acts in that way, it is to help you by removing from you all hope in this world and by urging you on toward Me who am your only goal" (*Dialogue*, Chap. 141). Passionately devoted to Providence, she spoke of it in unforgettable words. The realization that everything comes from love and returns to

143

love gave her an insight into the depths of God, filling her with ecstatic joy. Among the various sections of her *Dialogue*, the "Treatise on Providence" is so striking that for a long time the whole book was known by this title. Nor was this the only place in which she wrote about Providence. In her letters she often returned to it and she seemed to catch fire when she began to speak of it:

O most sweet will that gives life and banishes death, that gives light and puts darkness to flight! You destroy all the soul's afflictions and you make it grow strong with the perfume of virtues. You clothe it in the wedding garment, in the fire of divine love, and you make it partake of the food of God's glory and the salvation of souls at the table of the cross. . . . It follows that he who plunges his will in the Blood remains in perfect peace. There is no other way or means of tasting in this life the pledges of life eternal and of having it later as reward.

(Letter 359, to Leonardo Frescobaldi.)

The loving, holy will of God is everywhere: the soul sees that everything in this life, bodily ills as well as spiritual trials, happens for its good and through God's permission. His will rules everything and permits nothing that cannot be useful to us. Not even a leaf falls from a tree without the permission of Providence. How then can any of our trials fail to be bathed in a heavenly light? "When things displease us and do not go as we wish, we must assume and believe that they are pleasing to God" (Letter 294, to Sano di Maco and others). By abandoning itself to God's good pleasure the soul is united to Him, is clothed in His riches and becomes His spouse. "Being a bride means being of one will with one's husband. [The bride] can will only what [the husband] wills and it seems impossible to her to think differently from him" (Letter 221, to Sister Bartolomeo della Seta).

The soul derives many advantages from abandonment to God's will. First, it gains security:

> "The soul must keep itself humble, make My love its principle and its end, and, out of love, receive pleasure or displeasure as is pleasing to My will and not to its own. This is the rule to follow if you are not to be deceived and if you are to receive, with a love that is firmly founded on My will, everything that comes from Me, who am your end."
>
> (*Dialogue,* Chap. 68.)

The soul receives fervor also: "O sweet obedience, you make dead men live and run because you make [self-]will die; and the more it dies, the more rapidly does one run. The soul that is dead to the self-love of the fleshly will runs more lightly to unite itself to its heavenly Spouse by love" (Letter 217, to the Prioress and other Sisters of Santa Maria degli Angeli). Peace comes, too:

> Where is the tongue that can tell the peace of the faithful soul? Not that such a soul is always at peace, or that it is not exposed to the waves and the storms of the sea, but rather that its will is at peace because it is one with the will of God. For such a soul, storm is the same as calm because it is not anxious about itself. It serves its Creator, whether He wills it to be at war or at peace, and it loves peace as much as war and war as much as peace. For has it not seen in the light of faith, and hence does it not know, that both the one and the other come from the same love?
>
> (Letter 62, to Sano di Maco and others.)

Finally, the soul is given joy: "Therefore be content at all times and in all places because everything is given to us by eternal love" (Letter 10, to Benincasa, her brother Jacomo's son).

The loving soul finds God's will in every event that oc-

curs, for everything is a combination of "mystery and love."
That is why Catherine spoke of the reverence with which
we should receive all that happens, and that is also why she
did not wish anything to be regarded as unhallowed:

If you say to me: "I do not wish to be enslaved by temporal things,"
I shall answer that things are temporal only insofar as you wish them
to be. I have already told you that everything comes from the divine
goodness, and hence everything is good and perfect. I do not wish
you to despise effort on the pretext that things are temporal.

(Letter 30, to the Abbess of the Convent of
St. Martha in Siena and to Sister Niccolosa.)

Catherine also sought the will of God in the expressed will of
her superiors.

What does the soul need in order to find the riches of
divine transformation hidden in God's adorable will? It needs
light and effort. It learns from the cross "that God loves us
ineffably and desires only our good" (Letter 253, to Trincio
de' Trinci). Whatever happens to it or whatever it does, the
soul must keep its eyes fixed on this truth "like the eagle,
which, as it flies, looks at the sun and not the earth" (see
Letter 36, to some novices of the Order of Santa Maria di
Mont'Oliveto).

Then he who loves perfectly serves faithfully with a living faith. He
truly believes that whatever God gives or permits is given only to
sanctify us, for He does not will the death of the sinner but that he
be converted and live. The perfect lover has seen in the light of faith
that it is one and the same love that gives us great consolations,
permits the devil to torment us in spirit and allows creatures to persecute us. Hence he knows that God is sovereignly good and that only
a sovereign goodness can emanate from Him. He sees equally clearly
that nothing is done without God, save sin. That is why the faithful

soul embraces everything with love, since everything is good and is given us only for our salvation.

(Letter 62, to Sano di Maco and others.)

But man's will must also follow this light and abandon itself simply, yet completely and profoundly, to God's good pleasure. He must truly place his soul in the hands of his God. He will find strength to do so in contemplation, in the example of Him who made Himself obedient unto death and who, from His cross, calls us to obey Him and who in return gives us His peace: "Daughter, think of Me; if you do so, I shall immediately think of you" (*Life*, Part 1, Chap. 10).

17. The Way That Leads to Life

❖❖❖❖❖❖❖❖❖

HERE on earth, conformity to God's will necessarily pre-supposes patience because Providence leads us along the way of the cross. Hence Catherine used to say: "Without patience we cannot reach our beloved goal" (Letter 39, to Dom Jacomo, Carthusian). Patience is the best indication of the quality and soundness of our virtues and love. Without it, souls are like hollow trees, which produce some leaves and appear healthy enough but which give no fruit and are soon to die. As Catherine said so expressively, and so often, patience is "the core of charity": "The core of this tree—that is, of the love that is in the soul—is patience. It is the sign that I live in the soul and that the soul is united to Me" (*Dialogue*, Chap. 10).

Catherine was so deeply convinced of the importance and excellence of patience that, even in the privacy of a letter to her director, she burst out into a hymn of praise for the virtue:

O patience, how worthy of love you are! O patience, with what hope do you not fill those who possess you! O patience, you are a queen; you are always in command and are never the slave of anger! O patience, you treat sensuality as it deserves when anger causes it to

148

raise its head! You carry with you a two-edged sword, the sword of hatred and the sword of love, with which you strike and root out anger and pride, as well as impatience, the core of pride. The sun is your garment, shining with the light of true knowledge of God, burning with the heat of divine charity; and its rays, falling on those who persecute you, light coals that burn with a fire which charity fans and which sears and consumes the hatred in their hearts. Yes, O sweet patience born of charity, it is you who bear fruit in the neighbor and who glorify God. Your garment is sewn with stars, which are the various virtues, because you cannot live in a soul, O patience, without making the stars of all the virtues shine in the night of self-knowledge, which seems to be lighted only by the moon. And after this night of self-knowledge, day comes with the light and heat of the sun, which is your garment, O patience! Who would not fall in love with so sweet a thing as patience? Who would not love to suffer for Christ crucified?

Therefore, let us suffer, dearest and sweetest Father. Do not lose time! Strive to know yourself so that this queen may be the guest of your soul, for her presence is very necessary to you. It is the means of mounting the cross with Jesus crucified and of there sharing in His food. Behold that to which you are called and elected! When you are suffering, it will seem to be lighted only by the moon, but patience will give you the light of the sun.

(Letter 104, to Raymond of Capua.)

On the other hand, Catherine expressed her views on impatience briefly but definitely: "There is no vice or sin that gives us in this life such a foretaste of hell as anger and impatience" (Letter 38, to Monna Agnesa).

The mouth speaks from the fulness of the heart, and the Saint knew from experience the necessity and the value of the virtue of patience. A competent witness assures us that "if you tried to describe Catherine's patience, you would tarnish rather than praise it" (*Leggenda minore*, Part 3, Chap. 2).

Patience was one of the principal parts of the spiritual edifice which St. Catherine undertook to build. Actually, patience plays more than the negative role of defending the other virtues; it also helps us to acquire precious benefits by enabling us to derive infinite advantages from pain, which is inseparable from our condition as men. "This life does not pass without pain, and he who wishes to flee pain flees the reward without avoiding the pain" (Letter 76, to Frà Giovanni di Biondo). We would be on the wrong path if we wished to live our lives without encountering the cross: "Be careful, my beloved daughter, not to err," wrote Catherine to Monna Alessa:

You will be mistaken if you wish to eat at the Father's table and still wish to avoid the table of the Son. This is the table at which we must eat because nothing can be acquired without pain, and the Father cannot know pain, but only the Son. And since we cannot cross the stormy sea without pain, the sweet, tender Word who knows pain has marked out our way and our rule. He has prepared our path with His Blood.

(Letter 271.)

If this path seems hard, we can sustain our courage with the three following thoughts:

First, since He has given His life with so much love, we must be convinced that every pain, no matter whence it comes, and that all things, favorable or not, are given us out of love and not out of hatred, but for our good in order to make us reach the end for which we have been created.

(Letter 151, to Monna Nella di Bonconti.)

Then, so that we may avoid useless introspection and may view matters in the light of eternity, we should know that, no matter how great a pain may be, it is really very small since it is not greater than time and since, for us, time is no greater than the point of a needle. All our pains, therefore, are small and finite. We no longer have the pain that is past because time has taken it away. We have not yet had the pain that is to come, and it is possible that we shall not live to suffer it. Finally, having seen how short pain is, we should also see how useful it is. Ask that of the sweet and ardent St. Paul, who said to us that the sufferings of this life are not worthy to be compared with the glory to come which God has prepared for those who fear Him and who bear patiently the holy trials which the divine goodness sends them. He who does this tastes the pledges of heaven in this life by his patience.

(Ibid.)

Why, then, should we tremble? Rather "we should rejoice even under heavy burdens because, then, we receive the gift of strength" (Letter 344, to Raymond of Capua).

The loving soul finds even more advantages in patience. For us, as we make our way toward heaven, the cross is the birthplace and fatherland of love; it is there that the divine and the human unite: "Pain is no longer pain but, rather, consolation when we remember that it makes us share in the sufferings of Jesus crucified" (Letter 39, to Dom Jacomo, Carthusian). Since the cross is the instrument of redemption, our love of souls would be an empty love if it did not make us suffer for their salvation—a fact so evident that Catherine never ceases to speak of it: "We shall be eaters of souls at the table of the cross" (Letter 51, to Fra Felice da Massa); ". . . united to Him who, as if transported with love, ran to the ignominious death of the cross" (Letter 354, to Madonna Pentella [Pentesilea]).

Thus enlightened, humble patience becomes love of the cross: "Very often the soul whose virtue has not yet been tested is ready to suffer everything for its God; and when God sees that it has this desire, He tests it to see whether its love is real or mercenary" (Letter 335, to Dom Cristoforo, Carthusian). This being so, "it seems to me," Catherine confessed in a letter to Monna Alessa,

that my Spouse, who is Eternal Truth, has wished to test, in me and outside of me, visible and invisible things by a sweet, sure test, the invisible things being infinitely more numerous than those that are visible. But He has applied this test with such gentleness that my tongue could not describe it. So I wish that pains were my food, tears my drink and sweat my perfume. I wish that pains may make me strong, that pains may cure me, that pains may give me light, that pains may give me wisdom, that pains may clothe my nakedness, that pains may strip me of all self-love, both spiritual and temporal.

(Letter 119.)

On this level, the cross, which our weak human nature ordinarily regards as a sign of pain and death, becomes life and joy, because Christ is there and the soul surrenders itself to Him: "Rejoice with me upon the cross," cries St. Catherine, "and the cross will then become a couch upon which to rest, a table at which the food and the fruit of patience are tasted in peace and quiet" (*Ibid.*).

This attitude was so instinctive with Catherine that, no matter what trials she had to bear, a heartfelt cry of praise always rose from her lips: "May Christ the Lord be praised!" (*Life,* Part 2, Chap. 6). Her joy, even then, was so great that,

knowing and understanding the mystery of the divine will, she bore everything not merely with patience but even very willingly and with a joyful countenance, remembering the benefits that were to follow as a result. Her letters . . . clearly show that from the feast of the Circumcision [Jan. 1, 1380] until her blessed death [April 29], her soul was continually absorbed in thanking God for her torments, which she called "sweet," although she was extremely ill, and praying the Lord for the peace of Holy Church with zeal and love and a great abundance of tears.

(Leggenda minore, Part 3, Chap. 2.)

The Lord had taught her that the more [His servants] suffer, the more they rejoice. Even better, suffering every trial is for them an appeasement of the desire to die, and very often it is this very desire and will to suffer and bear pain that sweetens their painful desire to be delivered from their bodies.

(Dialogue, Chap. 84.)

Hence also comes the desire for reparatory and redemptive suffering, an infinite desire which encounters pain alone and which finds in it only an insufficient solace, for this is the mystery of joy and suffering experienced by Christ, a mystery which is echoed in the souls of the saints. Bowed under this weight, Catherine knelt in humble prayer:

Since that is not Your good pleasure, may Your will be done. But I beg You to deign to grant just one very small request. Since You have decreed that I am to remain some time longer in the flesh, allow me during that time to share in all the pains You bore, to the very last one.

(Life, Part 2, Chap. 6.)

153

18. Temptation

❖❖❖❖❖❖❖❖❖

SINCE sanctity is composed of love, peace and self-abandonment, would it not be sheer folly to attempt to attain it in the "world"? In fact, the world is not only incapable of fostering sanctity, but is animated by a completely contrary spirit—that corrupted and corrupting spirit cursed by Christ, who excluded it from His priestly prayer at the Last Supper. If we heed St. Bernard, we shall be fully convinced that salvation is to be found only by fleeing the world. Catherine, too, was aware of this: she had a high regard for the cloister and the religious life, she directed several of her disciples thereto, and when one of her converts gave her a castle near Siena, she even undertook the founding of a convent under the patronage of Mary, Queen of the Angels. But her own vocation was different. Putting her trust in the grace of Christ, she attacked the prince of the world on his own ground, which perhaps explains one of the most tragic aspects of her life, for the devil regarded her as "his enemy, his greatest enemy" (*Leggenda minore*, Part 2, Chap. 9), and harassed her relentlessly in soul and body.

Though well aware of the dangers and temptations of the world, Catherine was undaunted and, deep down, actually revelled in the battle, as she herself tells us: "It is not flight but rather combat that kills evil sentiments" (Letter 150, to Fra Francesco Tebaldi). The standard of the cross, under which she fought, was a pledge of victory over the world, the flesh and the devil, yet she remained on guard against the danger of presumption and over-confidence in self:

You ask me if I think I cannot be deceived by the devil. My answer is that, not only in this matter, which is beyond the powers of nature, but also in all my other actions, my weakness and the malice of the devil continuously fill me with fear. I believe that I can be in error because I know and see that the devil has lost eternal happiness but not his [angelic] intelligence, and I understand that, with this superiority of mind, he could easily deceive me. But I also take refuge in, and lean upon, the tree of the most holy cross of Jesus crucified. I cling to it and am convinced that if I remain fixed and nailed to it by love and humility, no devil can do anything against me, not because of my merits, but because of the merits of Jesus crucified.

(Letter 92, to a religious man in Florence.)

Moreover, we should not be afraid, because the citadel of the will is impregnable and neither God nor the devil can take it by force. Then, too, we can always have recourse to Jesus to strengthen our weakness:

O Word made flesh, You have made firm the stone which is the creature by cementing it to its Creator. By Your union with human nature, You have united the creature to God by Your Blood mixed with the quicklime of the Divine Essence. Thus You have made it able to resist contrary winds, attacks, temptations, and the pains that torment our souls, pains which come from the devil, from the creature and the flesh. Yes, I see, O Supreme Truth, that Your blood has surrounded us with a rampart so strong and so solid that no adverse wind can throw it down. Is not that a motive for the creature, O sweetest Love, to love only You and to fear none of the illusions that arise before it?

(Letter 36, to some novices of the Order of
Santa Maria di Mont'Oliveto.)

In another letter—to Pietro, Marchese di Monte—she wrote: "Armor is good, and He who aids us is still better. Nothing can resist God, and so long as the soul looks to this gentle, powerful Helper, it cannot fall into any weakness" (Letter 148).

Far from being injured by temptation, the soul derives precious benefit from it: "Virtue is acquired through that which is contrary to it," Catherine wrote to Blessed Raymond (Letter 211); "[temptations] make it reach its goal more quickly because the soul that feels that it is being attacked shakes off the sleep of negligence by hatred and knowledge of itself and by true humility" (Letter 84, to Fra Filippo di Vannuccio and Fra Niccolò di Piero). Through temptations we attain perfect love; and, at the risk of disconcerting us in our laxity, Catherine proclaimed what she had learned from God: "Therefore let the soul rejoice when it is tormented! That is the way to attain this sweet, glorious state" (*Dialogue*, Chap. 90). Furthermore, virtue grows and proves itself in battle. Finally, this law of human frailty keeps the soul truly humble. The frail body becomes for the soul a motive for humbling itself. It is "a fortunate rein which will restrain all inordinate vanity in you just as a rider tightens the rein on a bolting horse so that it will not go off the road" (Letter 237, to the Duke of Anjou). From the thorns of temptation, we draw "the sweet-smelling rose of perfect purity" when we resist (Letter 44, to Messer Antonio di Ciolo). Man knows himself better; "with holy hatred he stands up to his own frailty, and in humble, continual prayer, he searches lovingly for refuge in Christ crucified. And the more he clings to Him, the more he participates in His purity" (*Ibid.*).

How should we act in these battles so as to amass booty and become wealthy on the spoils of the enemy? In this matter, Catherine can give advice with the skill of a veteran who has experienced all the harshness of war. First, we need much energy and no discussion: "Follow the example of the very chaste woman who does not answer her would-be seducer when he speaks and who pretends not to hear him" (*Leggenda minore*, Part 1, Chap. 11). She herself had successfully adopted this uncompromising attitude toward the demon of impurity and during the severe temptations to discouragement that marked the beginning of her spiritual life. She used it also to overcome her natural repugnance while doing her heroic works of charity—for example, kissing a hideous sore "until she felt that the devil and her stomach had been completely dominated and conquered" (*Ibid.*, Part 2, Chap. 4). Because of her generous perseverance in such heroic gestures, her ardent recourse to prayer, and especially her conviction that she would find the will of God behind each trial, she was victorious in the battle. To the devil's threats she boldly replied:

I have chosen suffering as my refuge and I proclaim that I am happy to endure these and all other pains, no matter whence they come, for the love and glory of my Savior and dearest Spouse, in the manner and to the extent that shall please His goodness.

(*Ibid.*, Part 1, Chap. 11.)

She often repeats this recommendation:

Imagine that it will be the same with your soul, that it will be assailed by tumultuous thoughts. If it is conformed to the will of God and

157

sees that His love sends such thoughts to make its solicitude more perfect and its humility more sincere, it will find peace even when it is once again in the midst of battle.

(Letter 365, to Stefano Maconi.)

The main thing is to keep one's soul in peace so as to be able to give it to Christ: "Once man is master of himself, he is master of the whole world, for he is disturbed by nothing and fears nothing except God, whom he serves and loves" (Letter 259, to Tommaso d'Alviano).

Temptations are inherent in the Christian life, each state of life having its own, for there are temptations in solitude as well as in the world. Catherine knew all the temptations proper to her own vocation, and therefore she can guide us. Her parents were opposed to her intention of consecrating herself to Christ and did their best to prevent her from following her chosen way of life. But she was able to combine an unshakable resolve with the demands of obedience and due consideration for filial love. Thus, while she told her family that it would be easier to melt stones than to change her purpose, she also knelt humbly before her mother, whom she persuaded to allow her to take care of a repellent old woman.

Catherine knew that the world is a show place for false principles and biting criticism, for sin, scandal and seduction. But she also learned to throw the cloak of mercy over sins, to refrain from judging and, when faced with scandalous behavior, to pray God more fervently in order to obtain mercy and to compensate for the offense committed against Him. In her testament she said, "When confronted with an obviously sinful act, we should pity the sinner and pour out prayers before the Lord for him, but we should not feel disdain or contempt for the unhappy man" (*Life*, Part 3, Chap. 4). Even censure had become sweet to her: she used to say that "the devil takes possession of the hearts and tongues of his servants" (Letter 151, to Monna Nella di Bonconti). Far from being disturbed by criticism, she rejoiced in it: "This is my glory; this is what I want—to be well chewed during my life. And do not worry about it; let those who wish to talk, do so. That pains me for their sake, but not for my own" (*Fioretti*, p. 23).

Such things are all the better as mortifications because the soul has not chosen them itself: "If God sends you a cross, do not choose it by your own will but according to the will of Him who gives it to you" (Letter 187, to Dom Giovanni Sabbatini and Dom Taddeo de' Malavolti, Carthusians). When confronted with evils, the soul pours out before God a perfumed stream of humility and praise:

Lord, I am not surprised at men's waywardness. As for me, You have wounded my heart with Your perfect love; You have protected it by guarding its purity. Oh, if all those who are blinded by their senses and by pleasures had experienced the ineffable sweetness of Your holy love, it would have been impossible for them not to have detested immediately the shameful pleasures of the flesh! They would have run swiftly to quench their thirst at the fountains of Your sweetness.

(Caffarini, *Supplemento*, Part 2, Chap. 3.)

But we can add that the world also contains goods and pleasures that can shackle the soul; and since this is so, we must be wary and not presume on our strength. To Francesco di Filippo, Catherine wrote: "Do not rely on yourself, saying 'I am strong and am not afraid that they will make me fall.' No, for the love of God, do not say that!" (Letter 190).

Yet the loving soul can avoid this reef:

Here again is the reef of this world, of the deceptive world that

159

shows itself decked out with delights, with power and importance, and yet carries in it an undying bitterness. It is without constancy or stability; its joys soon vanish; it is like a flower that is beautiful and sweet-smelling when you pluck it in the field; but scarcely have you plucked it, when it loses its beauty and sweet odor and falls back into nothingness. The beauty and grandeur of the world are like a flower; as soon as the soul, out of inordinate love, seizes them, it finds them empty; their beauty has disappeared along with the perfume which they once possessed. They have this perfume because they have come from the holy mind of God, but they lose it very soon for him who gathers and clings to them with inordinate love. That is not their fault, nor is it the fault of the Creator who gives them to us, but rather the fault of him who has snatched them, who would not leave them in the place where they should be; that is to say, it is the fault of him who has not loved them for the glory and praise of God's name. Who avoids this reef? The obedient man in keeping the vow of voluntary poverty, for, as you see, there is no reef to be feared when you are sailing with the wind of true obedience.

(Letter 84, to Fra Filippo di Vannuccio and
Fra Niccolò di Piero.)

To paraphrase the letter she wrote to Dom Giovanni, of the Carthusian monastery in Rome: "The detached soul that seeks only God's good pleasure in everything will avoid this danger" (see Letter 201). When the will is upright, it is never separated from God, and the soul can easily find renouncement in pleasure. In this connection we are inevitably reminded of the way in which Catherine made her visit to the spa at Vignone an occasion for heroic mortification. Writing to Cardinal Bonaventura, she said: "Nobody can weaken [this strength] unless he consents to temptation by abandoning his strength, because there is no position or circumstance that can take God from us since God considers neither state nor place nor time but only sincere, holy desires" (Letter 334).

In one of the conversations that Catherine had with God, He Himself seemed surprised at, and proud of, the stability attained by the soul which nothing can harm:

"Oh, how happy this soul is! While still imprisoned in a mortal body, it tastes immortal things. It venerates everything. The left hand weighs no more heavily on it than the right; sorrows, no more than consolations; hunger and thirst, no more than eating and drinking; cold, heat and nakedness, no more than clothing; life, no more than death; praise, no more than vilification; fatigue, no more than rest. No matter what happens, it is unshakable, firm and stable; it is built upon the living rock. It has seen and known, with the light of faith and with firm hope, that everything has been given to you with one and the same end in view, with the same providence, since great trials are accompanied by great steadfastness. I always give only that which you are able to bear, when you desire to take upon yourself every affliction for love of Me."

(*Dialogue,* Chap. 141.)

Therefore, for the soul that wishes to walk this path, the whole secret is to lean upon faith and to find therein the strength of love that overcomes every obstacle. "Reflect on this," wrote Catherine to Fra Raymond:

The soul can neither receive nor desire virtue if it does not wish to bear persecutions and temptations with true, holy patience for love of Jesus crucified. We must, therefore, rejoice in struggles, afflictions and darkness since they are the source of so much virtue and joy.

(Letter 211.)

The Master made Catherine desire and ask for this strength before He exposed her to severe temptations and the dangers of the world. In reply to her prayer He taught her this exalted doctrine:

161

"Daughter, if you wish to acquire the virtue of strength, you must imitate Me. I could, by My divine virtue, annihilate the powers of the air or use any means whatsoever to triumph over them, and yet, with the purpose of giving you the actions of My humanity as an example, I willed to conquer by the way of the cross and to practice what My word taught you. Do you want to have strength to overcome every hostile power? Receive the cross as a solace for your heart. That is the way I received it. As My Apostle testifies, it was a great joy for Me to hasten to such a harsh and shameful cross. Choose pains and afflictions, not only by bearing them patiently, but also by embracing them as a consolation. And they truly are consolations because, the more you suffer them for Me, the more like Me you become. But if, through your sufferings, you bring your life into conformity with Mine, then, according to My Apostle's teaching, it will necessarily follow that you will also have to resemble Me in both grace and glory. Therefore, daughter, for My sake receive whatever is sweet as bitter and whatever is bitter as sweet, and do not doubt that then you will be strong in all circumstances."

(*Life*, Part 1, Chap. 11.)

When temptation, as violent and overpowering as a storm, was unleashed in Catherine, she used to exclaim: "I put my trust in our Lord Jesus Christ and not in myself" (*Ibid.*), and she would repeat to herself: "You will have all eternity to be consoled with Christ" (*Ibid.*). She understood "the mystery of these temptations" that are meant to unite us more closely with Christ. The Master appeared to His victorious young athlete to urge her on to new combats: "Do you see how much I have suffered for you? Therefore do not find suffering for Me too heavy a burden" (*Ibid.*).

"I am in the world but I am not of the world" (see John 17:11). This is the solution; we must not be wrapped up in self, but rather totally absorbed in God; instead of seeking self, we must no longer seek anything except to please Him:

Where is the tongue that is able to describe the peace of the faithful soul? . . . It is [the soul's] will that is at peace because it is one with God's will. Storm and calm are the same to it because it has no solicitude for itself. It serves its Creator whether He wills it to be at war or at peace, and it loves peace as much as war and war as much as peace. Has it not seen in the light of faith, and in seeing has it not known, that both the one and the other come from one and the same love?

(Letter 62, to Sano di Maco and others.)

19. Divine Friendship

❖❖❖❖❖❖❖❖❖

WHEN we see Catherine totally transformed in God and all on fire with love, we are moved to follow her. But how can we attain such heights? How can we acquire the love possessed by those who are perfect? The Saint herself replies, "By prayer and meditation upon divine love." She explains what she means in a letter to Fra Matteo dei Tolomei. Having reminded him of Peter's love, which, imperfect though it was at first, was perfected after he had received the fullness of the Holy Spirit, she adds:

The means of attaining thereto is the one used by the disciples—to shut oneself up in the house as did Peter and the others. That is what is and must be done by those who have attained the love of the Father and who are His sons. . . . We have said that they remained [there] for ten days and that then the Holy Spirit came. So the soul that wishes to attain this perfection must remain for ten days—that is, in the ten commandments of the Law. In addition to the commandments, it will follow the precepts because the two are bound together and the first are not observed without the second. . . . It is thus that we receive the fullness of the Holy Spirit, and this true wisdom comes from real enlightenment and perfect knowledge, as do the steadfastness and power that resist every attack.

(Letter 94.)

Catherine speaks from experience. In order to lead her to the heights of love, the Master had caused her to shut herself up for several years in rigorous silence and total retreat from the world—a silence which she scarcely broke except to go to confession, and a retreat which she never left except to go to church. Later, even during the most active years of her life, she still devoted long periods to prayer. In addition to the prayers imposed by the Dominican Third Order rule, she spent ecstatic hours after Communion and kept long night vigils during which she disregarded the demands of sleep. She also made much use of ejaculatory prayers, especially one which she was accustomed to say in her native language: "O God, come to my assistance! O Lord, make haste to help me!" (Ps. 69:2), an appeal which, Cassian tells us, the Fathers of the desert used to regard as the secret of continuous prayer. But, little by little, she had to abandon vocal prayer entirely, so that finally she could no longer say even an Our Father without going into ecstasy. This was the ardent prayer that obtained the great graces that dominated her life—the gift of fortitude, of faith, the mystical espousal and the exchange of hearts with our Lord.

It was thus she arrived at her sublime state of prayer. On countless occasions, those who approached her had the impression that "she was seeing with the eyes of her soul what was happening in heaven" (*Fioretti*, p. 21). She spoke with ease about the sublimest mysteries: thus when she referred to heaven, she described it as the place of the peace, light and life which the elect experience, which is perhaps the best indication of the heights she reached in contemplation. Nevertheless, she was almost tragically aware of the inadequacy of human language to describe what she saw:

If I used the poor words of our speech to tell what I have seen, it would seem that I was blaspheming God or that I was speaking against His glory, because there is such a difference between what the mind knows and understands in such an exalted manner, and what our inadequate words can say, that they would seem two completely opposite things.

(*Leggenda minore*, Part 2, Chap. 6.)

Hence, as we have said, when she speaks about prayer in all its forms, when she shows its importance and praises its advantages, she is speaking from experience. Vain is the love that does not make us thirst to be with God in the holy mystery of prayer, and vain the confidence that does not have recourse to Him. The all-embracing power of God implies, for us, the all-embracing nature of prayer. Catherine would have subscribed with all her heart to St. Teresa's words: "To give up prayer is to cast oneself into hell without the devil's help." Indeed, she herself said essentially the same thing, using a different metaphor:

Prayer is a pasture, a field in which all the virtues find their food, their growth, their vigor; and when they lack this resource, they grow feeble and die of hunger, as it were.

(Caffarini, *Supplemento*, Part 3, Chap. 2.)

To bring out the savor and utility of prayer, she used another figure of speech: "Prayer is a mother . . . who nurses at her breast her children, which are the virtues" (Letter 150, to Fra Francesco Tebaldi), because, as she explained elsewhere, "in holy prayer the soul finds all the treasures and all the joys that it can have in this life" (Letter 67, to the monks of Passignano).

According to Catherine, who in her usual ardent way echoed Christian tradition, prayer takes three principal forms.

First, there is *continual* prayer, "a holy desire and gentle impulse of love," which directs all our actions. In a lower degree, continual prayer is simply a "pure intention" by which we offer to God our activities: "We pray unceasingly by never ceasing to do good." But the soul that is striving to become "another Christ in a union of love" is not contented with this. It cannot, as it were, leave God's side even when it is engaged in its normal daily routine, and, like Catherine, it too builds "an interior cell within itself," a cell which it never leaves and in which it stays "alone and at peace" with God. "In making [this cell], the soul is working toward perfection; and no matter where it is or what persons it meets, it is always alone and at peace in [its cell]" (Caffarini, *Supplemento*, Part 3, Chap. 2). As the Saint once wrote: "[The soul] prays everywhere because it always carries with it the place in which God dwells by His grace and in which we should pray—that is, the cell of our soul, in which holy desire prays continually" (Letter 213, to Sister Daniella).

This is the stage at which the mystery of perfect love is achieved, the point where the soul, rising above its works, cares and fatigue to the full height of its love, is concerned solely with God, with thinking of Him and with pleasing Him; then, freely and trustingly, it rests in Him. "Think of me . . . and I shall immediately think of you," the Lord had said to Catherine (*Life*, Part 1, Chap. 10). When danger threatened during a sea voyage, she was surprised to find that Blessed Raymond was concerned about his safety and she asked him, "Why are you worried about yourself?" (*Ibid.*).

Continual prayer was one of the practices she most frequently recommended, as Raymond testifies:

I remember—it now comes back to me—that in the days when I was overburdened with exterior cares or when I had to travel, the holy virgin often used to repeat this advice to me: "Make in your soul an interior cell which you will never leave."

(*Ibid.*, Chap. 4.)

She used to emphasize the benefits of this advice by saying:

He who knows how to use the grace that the Lord places in everything that happens to us will continually profit. I want you to act thus in every event, happy or sad, and then, retiring into yourself, to say to yourself: "I wish to derive some benefit from this." If you do so, you will soon be rich.

(*Life*, Part 2, Chap. 5.)

Prayer such as this, giving the soul security and life with God even here on earth, is the summit to which the whole life of prayer should lead.

Then there is *vocal* prayer, which is intended solely to help the soul raise itself toward God. On this subject, the Saint stressed two points in particular—fidelity and adaptability. First of all, fidelity is essential. In fact, the devil often does his utmost to turn the soul away from its exercises of piety on the pretext that they are imperfect, useless or excessively rigorous. But he who wishes to give himself to Christ must persevere in his exercises of devotion, aware that to give them up would be "to expose oneself to all kinds of wretchedness" (Letter 84, to Fra Filippo di Vannuccio and Fra Niccolò di Piero). Then there is adaptability. The prayer of the lips is meant only to help that of the heart and should be left aside when it no longer serves its purpose. This, of course, does not apply where prayers of obligation are concerned; for example, saying the Divine Office. The soul should then be silent and attentive to God as soon as He comes to it. This part of the Saint's advice is extremely important, coinciding as it does with St. Thomas' teaching on the gifts of the Holy

Spirit. Docility in prayer makes the soul alert to receive the wisdom of love; and if it rejects this unction, it will become dry and arid. Catherine was not unacquainted with these periods of aridity, those somber hours in which the whole spiritual life is darkened. At such times she recommended the soul to persevere humbly, to trust calmly in God and to kneel before the crucifix, saying simply: "Jesus, Jesus, I trust in our Lord Jesus Christ!" (Letter 4, to a Carthusian monk).

Finally, there is *mental* prayer, the soul of vocal prayer and the mainstay of continual prayer, which would die without it just as a fire dies if it is not fed with fuel. For Catherine, mental prayer is "the mother of virtues," since it conceives and bears them. Because it is, as it were, the soul of sanctity, all the forces of the devil and our fallen nature are arrayed against it. The devil knows that it is the principal stronghold of man's resistance and that it puts the strength of God in His children's arms, while nature feels that mental prayer is the strongest opponent of worldly inclinations and instincts. Catherine, who had long observed this, insisted particularly on perseverance and fervor in prayer.

For the rest, we have something even better than her directions to lead us in the ways of mental prayer: we have her own living, ardent example to follow. By great good fortune we possess something that is quite unusual in the history of the saints, for, as we saw, we have her very own prayers, taken down by her secretaries as she prayed aloud in ecstasy. One word suffices to describe these prayers perfectly: they are *genuine*. In them, there is no affectation or stiffness on the one hand, or over-familiarity on the other; they are simply the words of a creature, conscious of her nothingness, speaking to her Creator and going beyond visible things to soar upward toward God the eternal. In them, too, there is ardent love and an absolute confidence in Him who loves us to excess. They are beautiful examples of that prayer "in spirit and in truth" which God the Father desires. We can view Catherine's prayers from several aspects, but the one that immediately strikes us and excites our wonder is the simplicity of her gaze upon God. There is no preoccupation with self here, none of that self-analysis of a soul that is thinking of itself and weighing its progress in God's sight. Catherine is concerned solely with God and His mysteries; the Trinity, the Incarnation, the Redemption, eternal life and the needs of the Church are all she contemplates in the divine light. Seen from this point of view, her prayer was genuine in its breadth; that is to say, it had become infinite, embracing the whole Church and all the world, and if sometimes it focused on a particular object, it retained its same amplitude of desire by reason of the things she prayed for. She desired and asked for what God thirsts to give—whence came her bold confidence, which did not rest on her own merits, for she knew her own nothingness, but rather on God, who loves His creatures and is almost foolishly eager to shower His gifts on them. Are not these the spiritual characteristics of true prayer—a gaze lost in God, an absorbing interest in His glory, a tapping of the infinite power of God's fatherly mercy, a human echo of the divine *Pater noster?*

Such prayer enlightens the soul and makes it keenly aware of the truths of faith. By abasing itself, the soul discovers truth because, as Catherine herself remarked, "if we wish to see the stars which are God's mysteries, let us descend into the deep well of His humility" (Letter 343, to Rainaldo of Capua). There, too, the soul finds divine strength; it is then in God, in whom it finds and can do everything: "I will go as far as you," God had said to her.

Above all, prayer is love because, more than anything else, God's love entrances the soul which cannot contemplate it without being captivated by it: "When the soul sees that it is so greatly loved, how can it resist loving in return? It simply cannot" (Letter 44, to Messer Antonio di Ciolo). Catherine was also insistent in recommending a thirst for enlightenment because if the soul becomes more enlightened, its love will increase, and if its love increases, so will its virtues and good works up to the moment of death: "All the coldness of our hearts comes solely from the fact that we do not consider how much God loves us" (Letter to 279, to Ristoro Canigiani).

God's love is the divine attribute which should most fascinate the soul. This is St. Catherine's whole thought, her whole life—believing in God's love so ardently that faith becomes vision, a vision to which the soul responds with love. No one has extolled so much as she the captivating and sanctifying power of God's love when it is contemplated by the soul. Outside this love the soul dies:

You will find this source of love in the side of Christ crucified, and that is where I wish you to seek your refuge and your abode. Know that the religious outside his cell dies like the fish out of water, and I speak to you about the cell in Jesus' side, where you will find knowledge of yourself and of His goodness.

(Letter 36, to some novices of Santa Maria di Mont' Oliveto.)

This is the secret of Catherine's sanctity; the whole mystery of God's love plunged her into an ecstasy. She regarded divine love as the source of all things, as she confided to Fra Bartolomeo Dominici:

I invite you to enter a deep, untroubled ocean by means of this very ardent love. . . . Not that this ocean is new but what is new is my soul's appreciation of the truth "God is love." Just as the mirror reflects a man's face and the sun sheds its light on the whole earth,

so this truth shows my soul that all of His works are all love because they come solely from love, and He Himself says, "I am God-Love."
(Letter 146, to Fra Bartolomeo when he was a lector in Florence.)

She marvelled at God's goodness in creating us to His own image and likeness: "It is therefore the fire of love that urges Him to create us in His own image and likeness. He creates [men] in a dignity so great that no tongue can describe or eye envisage or heart surmise the dignity of man, so great is it" (Letter 21, to an unnamed person). And, finally, she praised the mercy of God, which causes Him to love us despite our sins:

You saw in Your divine light all the crimes Your creature was to commit, and You acted as if You did not see them. You fixed Your eyes on Your creature's beauty, with which You are almost foolishly entranced. . . . Yes, love makes You create us despite the fact that You foresee our offenses. You persist in Your love because You are wholly a furnace of love.

(Prayer 5.)

However, Catherine drew her knowledge of God's love mainly from meditation on the Passion of Christ. Not only did her body bear invisibly the fiery stigmata but her soul also carried the marks of the Passion in the form of love. A witness relates that "she spoke of [the Passion] with such telling effect that she seemed to be describing something she had actually experienced rather than heard about" (*Leggenda minore*, Part 2, Chap. 6).

The feature of the Passion that most captivated her was the wound in Christ's side, that wound which reveals the secret of His heart, which shows us that His infinite love remained unsatisfied because finite suffering could not exhaust it. More than once she thought that her heart had entered the Savior's side and had become one with Christ's own heart. At such times she felt her soul melt completely under the radiance of divine love, so that she cried out: "Lord, You have wounded my heart! Lord, You have wounded my heart!" (*Life*, Part 2, Chap. 6). In the wound in Christ's side, she found herself inebriated with the Precious Blood, "that Blood which gives life and makes visible what is invisible" (Letter 55, to Dom Guglielmo, Abbot General of the Carthusians), that Blood which contains all remedies, all strength and all sweetness. So keenly was she aware of Christ's immense love that when she could not find words to express it adequately, she invented one and used it as the signature of her soul and the seal of her doctrine: "Jesus-Love."

She invited everyone to drink at, and to take refuge in, the source of life: "Bathe in the Blood of Jesus crucified; hide yourself in His sweet, His most sweet wounds; and there expand, consume your heart" (Letter 48, to Matteo, son of Giovanni Colombini, of Siena). "Become inebriated with the Blood, satiate yourself with the Blood, clothe yourself in the Blood. . . . In time of battle you will find peace, and in bitterness you will find sweetness" (Letter 102, to Raymond of Capua). But why pile quotation upon quotation? If we were to transcribe them all, "we should have to copy at least a good fifth of her works," as Papini says.

The call of love is addressed to all souls because the words of love are written in letters so large that everyone can read them: they are "written in the Blood, and the initials are the most sweet and most sacred wounds of Christ" (Letter to John of Parma). The soul that discovers divine love has only to gaze fixedly at it and allow itself to be consumed by its fire, "the fire mingled with the Blood" (*Ibid.*).

20. The Sacraments of Union

❖❖❖❖❖❖❖❖❖

THE Christian soul, therefore, need only set out to seek God. Yet finding Him would have been impossible if He had not built a bridge between His heaven and our earth by sending us His Son made man. Therefore we must use this "bridge" to cross the great abyss and to possess finally the only good that satisfies our cravings. All of us Christians are bound to undertake the crossing and, according to St. Catherine, if we are to progress from sin to sanctity by means of the bridge, which is the only route possible, we must go through three stages, each of which is symbolically marked on the body of Christ.

At the outset, the soul's love is mercenary; it serves Christ for the sake of the benefits it finds in His service. Its union with Him is imperfect, for it has reached no further than His feet. But as it makes progress in stripping away self-love and in meditating upon its Creator's infinitely generous love, it reaches Christ's heart and enters the mystery of pure love. But it can go still higher, until it comes to His lips, where it receives the kiss of peace and is totally transformed. But the bridge that is Christ is a long one, and the pilgrims who set out across it may fall by the wayside. However, the Divine Architect has provided for that, for on it He has built an inn in which they can find shelter and "in which . . . the Bread and the Blood are distributed so that My creatures who pass by as travellers may not be overcome in the course of their lives" (*Dialogue*, Chap. 27). Or, in plain words, Christ calls all men to sanctity by union with Him; He has instituted His Church so that they can find in it all the help they need in their immense undertaking, the principal aid being the Eucharist, the Bread that gives strength and the Wine that inebriates.

Catherine had personal experience of this, too, for when she had come out of her solitude and had begun to spend herself for souls, she had felt irresistibly drawn toward the Blessed Sacrament. No doubt God, who had been so sinned against, wished in this way to console and sustain her whom He had destined to live in the midst of the world as He did and for His sake. An unceasing shower of graces proved to her the fathomless wisdom of God's apparent folly. Doubtless the outpouring of grace was meant to supply the needs of her soul and to show her God's merciful predilection for her, but it was also the reward for her faithful answer to the divine call. It is almost impossible for us today to understand the persecution, mockery and calumny to which she was exposed because of her frequent reception of Holy Communion. She was advised by some, and forbidden by others, to receive as frequently as she did, and she was publicly refused Communion in an attempt to make her abandon the practice; but her only reply was to trust more than ever in the instincts of her heart and the love which drew her to the Eucharist.

For her services to the Holy See, which were at times heroic, she asked only one reward: the privilege of receiving the Heavenly Bread more frequently and more easily. In a papal bull, Gregory XI granted her "the privilege of the portable altar and authorization to receive Communion whenever she pleased and without obtaining permission from anyone" (*Leg-*

genda minore, Part 2, Chap. 12). The Blessed Virgin gave her as confessor a true disciple of St. Thomas Aquinas to support and encourage her in her love for frequent Communion. As Blessed Raymond of Capua himself plainly tells us, this was one of the reasons that led the Saint to choose him as her spiritual director. Accordingly, she must often have spoken to him, in his role as a revered guide, about her cherished secret and the divine enlightenment she found in daily Communion, in which she saw Christ in all the mysteries of His life—as a smiling infant, as a youth, as the Shepherd of souls, as a bleeding Victim and a glorious Victor. From the Eucharist she ascended to the Trinity, there to contemplate the "Three Faces in one single Substance" (*Ibid.*) and to see the relationships between the Divine Persons in other symbolical forms. As the Eucharistic veil parted, she discovered the immense divine fire capable of consuming every soul. She shared in the angels' adoration and in our Lady's worship of her Son. What more is there to say? It was as if, for her, faith had given way to clear vision. Furthermore, each Communion threw her into a heavenly ecstasy which lasted two or three hours and in which her soul was flooded with peace, completely ravished and inebriated with a heavenly delight that made every earthly joy tasteless in comparison. Her soul, overwhelmed by so much love, could only echo the words which God spoke to her: "There is not even one creature whose heart would not melt with love as it contemplates, among all the other benefits you have received from Me, the benefit of this sacrament" (*Dialogue*, Chap. 11).

Yet we must remember that these graces were, in part at least, God's answer to her prayers. As far as it is possible for a creature to prepare itself to receive its Creator, her preparation for Communion was worthy of her Divine Guest. "O Father, I hunger!" she used to murmur in the eagerness of her desire;

"If you only knew how I hunger!" Hunger is both the awareness of the need to restore one's strength and the desire for the
food that has been prepared—all of which tortured the Saint.
She looked deep into her heart and then fled to God with
ardent desire, so that her Communions became so many
moments of heaven, light, joy and divine transformation. She
expounded her teaching on this matter in a letter to Ristoro
Canigiani in which we feel she was speaking from experience.
The following extensive quotation from that letter is really a
description of what a truly holy and sanctifying Communion
should be:

I am going to answer you on the subject of Holy Communion and tell
you how we should receive it. We should not indulge in foolish
humility as worldly people do. I mean that we should receive this
sweet sacrament because it is the food of the soul, food without which
we cannot live in the state of grace. Hence no bond is so strong that
it cannot and should not be broken in order to come to this sweet
sacrament. On his part, man must do what he can, and that is sufficient. And how ought we to receive Communion? In the light of the
most holy Faith and with the mouth of holy desire. In the light of
the most holy Faith, you will see in the Host the whole God and the
whole man. Then the intellect will lovingly receive the love that
results from its considerations, and it will piously meditate upon its
own defects and sins. Thus the soul is led to contrition. It wonders
at the greatness and the unfathomable charity of God, who, with so
much love, has given Himself as our food. And if it seems to the soul
that it is not at all in the state of perfect contrition and as perfectly
disposed as it would wish, let it not forego [Holy Communion] because good will is enough for it and, so far as it is concerned, it
possesses those dispositions which it should have.

I wish to add that it is desirable to partake of this food as it is
prefigured in the Old Testament, where it is laid down that the lamb
should be roasted and not boiled, whole and not cut up, that the

entrails be burned, that [those who partake of it do so] standing, with staffs in their hands, and that the blood of the lamb be poured out on the threshold of the door. That is the way in which we should receive this sacrament. We should eat the lamb roasted and not boiled; for if it is boiled, it is placed in earth and in water, that is to say, in earthly affection and in the water of self-love, whereas when it is roasted there is no intermediary between it and the fire. To eat it roasted therefore signifies taking it to the fire of divine love. Moreover, we should gird ourselves with the girdle of conscience because it would be shameful to approach perfect Purity with unclean hearts and bodies. We should be standing; that is to say, our hearts and souls should be faithful and completely turned toward God, and we should hold the staff of the most holy cross, from which we draw the doctrine of Christ crucified. That is the staff upon which we lean and which defends us from our enemies—the world, the flesh and the devil. We should eat it whole and undivided, which signifies that, with the light of faith, we must consider in this sacrament not only the humanity but also the body and soul of Christ crucified, united and merged with the Deity—the whole God and the whole man. Finally we should take the blood of this Lamb and put it on our foreheads; that is, we should confess it before every rational creature and never deny it out of fear of suffering or death. That is the way in which you should eat this Lamb—roasted in the fire of charity upon the wood of the cross. And thus we shall be marked with the sign of Tau and shall not be struck down by the destroying angel.

I have told you that we should not act, and I do not wish you to act, like so many foolhardy worldly people who break the commandments of Holy Church. "I am not worthy," they say. And so they spend long days in mortal sin, refusing the food of their souls. Oh, what absurd humility! Who does not see that you are not worthy? You say you are waiting for the time when you will be worthy. When will that be? Do not wait, because you will not be any more worthy on the last day than you were on the first. Even if all our actions are good, we shall never be worthy. But God is the one who is worthy and who, with His own great worth, makes us worthy. And His worth cannot decrease. But as for us, what should we do? We should prepare ourselves to keep the sweet commandment because, if we do not do so and neglect Communion, then, thinking that we shall avoid sin, we shall fall into it.

Therefore, to conclude, I do not want to see such folly in you but rather that you dispose yourself, as a faithful Christian, to receive Holy Communion in the manner I have just described. The more you possess true self-knowledge, the more perfection you will bring to this act because, with self-knowledge, you will see everything in its true light. May your holy desire never be dimmed by pain or injury, by the wrongs or ingratitude of those whom you have served; but rather may you, like a man and with true, unflagging tenacity of purpose, persevere unto death. And I pray you so to act, for the love of Jesus crucified.

(Letter 246.)

The soul that receives Communion in this manner immerses itself in Christ and lives in Him as the fish lives in the sea. It receives the intoxicating sweetness and the invincible strength of the redeeming Blood. It is able to bear all the fatigues of the climb to sanctity, and, little by little, it is changed into Christ in a spiritual transubstantiation that is the goal of the sacramental transubstantiation: "It is now no longer I that live, but Christ lives in me" (Gal. 2:20).

21. "Baptism in the Blood"

THE pilgrims who cross the bridge, hoping to receive from Christ the grace of union with Him, find that the holy inn provides not only food to sustain them but also balm for their wounds, for the Blood of Christ is both food and medicine. Next to the Eucharist, the sacrament of penance is the sacrament of the love that pardons and purifies, the sacrament of the mercy that draws good from evil; and it is to penance that Catherine next turns her thoughts. In speaking of penance, she uses words that express vividly the depths of purity, the forces for renewal, the rebirth of innocence and life, the resurgence of vigor and joy that are to be found in this sacrament: "baptism in the Blood" (*Dialogue*, Chap. 75); "baptism in the spirit" (Prayer 3). And often, when referring to penance, she merely repeats the formula: "Love to cleanse the face of your soul from all stain of sin in the Blood of Christ" (Letter 358, to Andrea di Vanni).

Baptism in the Blood! All that the Saint tells us about the Precious Blood; all her eager longing and childlike trust, her tragic awareness of her powerlessness to answer God's call adequately, and her generous resolve to respond as well as she can; all she felt within her at the solemn, intimate moment when she knelt to receive Christ's pardon—all this is hinted at in this phrase. We say it is only hinted at because her confessor, Blessed Raymond, merely alludes to it in general.

She went to confession often and accused herself unsparingly. Her sorrow was particularly keen because, as she knew, we receive the merits of the Precious Blood in proportion to our dispositions and contrition especially. The Precious Blood purifies and embellishes our souls only in proportion to the horror we have of sin, a horror which Catherine felt so intensely that even after six centuries we can still appreciate her poignant emotion when, in the midst of her most sublime ecstasies, her cry, "I have sinned, Lord, have mercy on me!" (Prayer 1), bursts out like a sob. On one occasion, as we have seen, when she thought she had lied because she had inattentively consented to a request which she could not grant, she wept inconsolably for three days. And on another occasion she felt "a mortal shame" at having allowed herself to be distracted for a moment from a divine vision, as Caffarini attests. What a perfect example of pure, virginal love in the blinding light of essential sanctity!

Confession should be, in addition, an effective means of avoiding that tepidity which, unfortunately, always threatens us here on earth, where sanctity remains so fragile, so subject to vicissitudes. But when we approach penance with fervor, the Precious Blood keeps us alert and free of the danger of falling asleep because of slackness or negligence. The redeeming Blood turns evil into good, sin into grace, offenses into love; and, as on the day it was first shed, it continues to change thieves into saints.

22. The Queen of the Apostles

THERE was once a woman in Lombardy who led a retired life and had great devotion to our Lady. When she heard that a new Order of Preachers had been founded, she ardently desired to see some of them. Now it happened that Friar Paul and a companion passed through that district preaching. The two of them went to visit her and, as was the Friars' custom, they spoke to her about the things of God. She asked them who they were and to what order they belonged, to which they replied that they were Friars Preachers. The woman, seeing that they were young, good-looking and becomingly dressed, despised them because she thought that men like them, going about in the world as they did, could not preserve their purity very long. However, the following night, it seemed to her that the Blessed Virgin came to her, with sadness in her face, and said to her: "You offended me gravely yesterday. Do you think that I cannot preserve my servants, despite their youth, in their journeys through the world for the salvation of souls? Well, then, to convince you that I have taken them under my protection, I am going to show you those whom you despised yesterday." And drawing aside her cloak, she showed the woman a great multitude of friars, among them being the ones whom she had judged so harshly. The repentant recluse was deeply devoted to the Friars from that moment on, and she related to others what had happened.[1]

[1] *Il Libre d'Oro Domenicano*, an anonymous 15th century translation of *Vitae Fratrum*

After the Annunciation, the Blessed Virgin had hastened to help her cousin Elizabeth and to share her own happiness with her. In much the same way, there are close bonds between Mary and those who travel the roads of the world in search of lost sheep. Instinctively we recognize our Lady's presence in Catherine's life by that calm, pure beauty that enveloped her, for her whole existence was, like each of her letters, dedicated to "the name of gentle Mary."

Even when she was a child, the Hail Mary had blossomed on the Saint's lips, leaving there a sweet perfume. Later, she turned to the Virgin of Virgins, confiding her desire never to have any spouse but the Son of God and placing her virginity in Mary's hands. And thirteen years later, on the occasion of the mystical marriage, our Lady was present and "took Catherine's hand in her own holy hand and, presenting her to the Son, sweetly invited Him to espouse her in the faith" (*Life*, Part 2, Chap. 11). Mary was present, also, in the secrecy of Catherine's cell and never left her during the days of her public life; Catherine tells us, too, that our Lady, "with her own most holy hands, began to knead the miraculous bread with her" (*Life*, Part 2, Chap. 11). Even more, it was Mary who provided her with the father and wise counsellor whom she needed so much, as she often reminded him in her letters by calling him, "Father, you whom sweet Mary gave me" (Letters 373 and 211, to Raymond of Capua). This was the secret of the Saint's closeness to her spiritual guide. In fact, we get the impression that in no other part of Catherine's correspondence was our Lady's influence so marked as in her letters to Raymond. To quote her own words to him, "First of all, keep to your cell in the presence of Mary and before the holy cross, in holy, humble prayer, in true self-knowledge, in

O.P., by Fra Gérard de Frachet, O.P., ed. by P. Innocenzo Taurisano (Rome: Ferrari, 1925), pp. 49-50.

living faith and the will to suffer" (Letter 267, to Raymond
of Capua). And elsewhere she advises him: "On every occasion have recourse to Mary and embrace the holy cross."

Ever aware of the power of our Lady's intercession, she
sometimes slipped into a letter to a sinner who was resisting
her this variation on her conclusion: "Sweet Jesus, Jesus-Love!
Mary, sweet Mother!" (Letter 21, to an unnamed person).
When she wrote to the prostitute in Perugia in an attempt to
persuade her to change her life, she said gently:

And do not think that this will be beyond your strength. Have recourse to sweet Mary, who is a merciful mother; she will lead you
into the presence of her Son and, for your sake, will show Him the
breast that suckled Him and will ask Him to have mercy on you.
Then you, who are His daughter and slave redeemed at the price
of His Blood, hide yourself in the wounds of the Son of God. There
you will find the fire of that ineffable love that can burn away and
totally erase all your misery.

(Letter 276.)

We need not be surprised, then, at the way Catherine
envisaged the mystery of Mary. First of all, for her our Lady
was a secure refuge in every difficulty: "On every occasion
have recourse to Mary" (Letter 267, to Raymond of Capua).
To her she confided all her requests:

O Mary, I have recourse to you! To you I present my prayer for the
sweet spouse of your very dear Son and for His Vicar on earth. . . .
I pray also for those whom you yourself have recommended to my
desires with a love of predilection. Inflame their hearts and do not
allow their fervor to die down. May they be like coals ever glowing
in the fire of your charity, and may they be consumed for you and
their neighbor. Thus in the time of trial may they have their ships
well rigged and provisioned for themselves and others. I pray for

those whom you have given me. . . . Today [the feast of the Annunciation] I boldly beseech you because it is a day of graces, and I know, O Mary, that nothing can be refused you.

(Prayer 11.)

Mary is the dispenser of fire, the mother of fair love. How then could Catherine, thirsting with love, help turning to her?

Mary is our advocate, the mother of grace and mercy. She is not ungrateful to those who serve her; she never forgets and always rewards them. She is like a fiery chariot because she conceived within her the Word, the only-begotten Son of God. She carries and spreads the fire of love because her Son is love.

(Letter 184, to the Prior and friars of the
Company of the Virgin Mary.)

Catherine found also in Mary a profound union with the mystery of the Redemption and the cross:

The Son was stricken in His body, and the mother was, too, because He was her flesh. It was truly just that she should suffer in that which belonged to her because it was in her womb that He had taken her spotless flesh. O fire of love! I see another resemblance: the Son has the form of the flesh; but the mother, like hot wax, has received the imprint of the desire for and love of our salvation from the seal of the Holy Spirit, and it was by means of this seal that the Divine Word became flesh. The mother, like a tree of mercy, received within her the ardent soul of her Son, who was stricken and wounded by the Father's will, and, like a tree that has a graft upon it, she also was wounded by the sword of love and hate. Hatred and love increased so much in the mother and the Son that the Son ran to meet death. His ardor sacrificed His life for us; His hunger and thirst to obey His Father were so great that He lost His love of

185

self and embraced the cross. His sweet, tender mother did likewise: she willingly sacrificed the love of her Son to such an extent that not only did she, tender as she was, not wish to save Him from death but was also prepared to act as a ladder by which He could ascend the cross. This is not surprising, because the love of our salvation had wounded her like an arrow.

(Letter 30, to the Abbess of the Convent of St. Martha in Siena and to Sister Niccolosa.)

Going beyond this human point of view, Catherine loved to salute Mary as the temple of the Trinity, associated with the master plan and work of the Triune God. Hence sprang the Saint's feeling of "sweetest love" for our Lady. The words of praise that rose from Catherine's heart when, on the feast of the Annunciation, she contemplated this event in Mary's life, clearly reveal the secret of her soul:

O Mary, Mary, temple of the Trinity! O Mary, bearer of fire! Mary, minister of mercy! Mary, mother of the divine fruit! Mary, redemptress of the human race because it was by your flesh suffering in the Word that the world was redeemed! O Mary, ocean of tranquility! O Mary, giver of peace! O Mary, fertile soil! O Mary, you are the new stem that produced the perfumed flower, the Word, the only begotten of God. It was in you, the fertile soil, that the Word was sown. You are the soil and you are the stem! O Mary, fiery chariot that carried the fire hidden and veiled under the ashes of your humanity! O Mary, vessel of humility, in you shone and burned the light of true knowledge that raised you above yourself to the point of entrancing the gaze of the Eternal Father, who snatched you up, lifting you toward Himself in a surge of love and predilection. Through this light, through the fire of your love, through the suffering of your humility, you drew His divinity to you and caused it to descend upon you although, it is true, He had already been urged to come to us by the most ardent fire of His incomprehensible charity. . . . Thus, Mary, you have become the book in which our rule is written. Today the wisdom of the Eternal Father is engraved in you; today man's power and freedom is demonstrated. . . . O Mary, I see the Word that was given to you, I see that He is in you. . . . O Mary, blessed be you among all women, world without end!

(Prayer 11.)

Catherine was able to find in our Lady an example for every occasion, a sure sign of her tender love for the Mother of God. Once when she wished to teach Monna Lapa, her mother, the detachment demanded by the life of an apostle, she answered Lapa's impatience at her delay in returning to Siena by saying:

I want you to learn a lesson from Mary, that sweet mother, who, for the glory of God and our salvation, gave her Son to die upon the wood of the holy cross. When Mary was left alone after Christ's ascension into heaven, she lived with the holy disciples; and, granted that this was a great consolation for her as well as for them, their departure must have been a great sorrow. Nevertheless, for the glory and praise of her Son and for the good of the whole world, she consented to it and wished them to leave. Only her love for God's glory and our salvation made her prefer the pain of their departure to the consolation of their remaining. I want you to learn from this example, dearest mother.

(Letter 240, to Monna Lapa.)

Finally, she found confidence in Mary. Not that our Lady is ever ungrateful, but her gratitude must be understood in its true sense as applying to supernatural things. The Saint knew that our devotion to Mary must not consist in words or sentiments but that it should be real, composed of efforts and virtues: "I also beg you to hate and have a horror of the sin of impurity and all other sins because it would not be fitting for you to defile yourself while serving Mary who is purity

187

itself" (Letter 184, to the Prior and friars of the Company of the Virgin Mary).

That is the essential point: union with Mary exists only to help us to surrender ourselves to the demands of divine love. When Catherine was slightly distracted during a vision, our Lady reproved her and inspired her with "a mortal shame" for her discourtesy, as Caffarini tells us. Mary is ever the mother of the Spouse who inundates His beloved spouses with His purity and wraps them in His jealousy—a jealousy that is, however, due to His special love. She wishes to lead each soul to her, so that each will surrender itself to that intimacy with God which means "becoming to Him like another self through a union of love."

Part 4. *The Church*

＊＊＊＊＊＊＊＊

23. Love of the Church

❖❖❖❖❖❖❖❖❖

IF WE are to understand both Catherine's mind and message, we must study her love of the Church, a love which
was the inspiration of all her writings, the source of their
truth and broad scope. She lived according to God's command: "Therefore, consecrate your life, your heart and your
love solely to this Spouse [Christ's Church], for My sake and
without any thought of self" (Letter 371, to Raymond of
Capua). She believed and taught that we must love the Church
passionately for the love of Jesus crucified. She called the
Church "the sweetness of her soul," a phrase that reveals the
depth of her appreciation of God's love in the mystery of the
Church. On the one hand, she saw in the Church the revelation of Christ's love, and hence she meditated often on the
Church as His "Spouse," a term which expresses exactly our
Lord's love for His Church. More frequently still, she loved
to regard the Church as the dispenser of the fruits of the
Redemption, as the wine cellar in which the precious vintage
of Christ's Blood is stored. On the other hand, she was utterly
convinced that we can do nothing for the salvation of our
neighbor except by building up the Church, the Mystical
Body into which Christ incorporates us.

Two passages selected from her letters will express force-

191

fully these two aspects of her thought; but to understand her mind, we must remember that, as we have mentioned already, her phrase "the Mystical Body of Holy Church" should be translated into modern terminology as "the Mystical Body that is Holy Church."

The Saint was aware that she was to die soon, and the last weeks of her life were filled with new lights and more ardent desires for the good of the Church:

The crucified desire that I had recently conceived in the presence of God has plunged me into an agony of pain because my mind, fixed upon the Trinity, sees in that divine abyss the dignity of the rational creature, the wretchedness into which mortal sin casts men, and the needs of Holy Church which God showed me in His bosom. But no one can taste the beauty of God in the abyss of the Trinity without the intervention of this Spouse [the Church], because all must pass through Christ crucified, who is the door, a door which is found only in Holy Church. Hence I saw that this Spouse distributes life (and there is in her so much life that no one can do her to death); I saw that she gives strength and light, that no one can weaken her or darken her innate brightness and that the fruit which she must bear, far from ever being lacking, increases continually.

(Letter 382, to Raymond of Capua.)

The second quotation from her letters shows the necessary bond that exists between the work of the apostolate and the endeavor to build up the Mystical Body. We know that this letter was written several years before because in it there is mention of the Florentine war, and it was addressed to Niccolò da Osimo, an important dignitary in the Papal Curia.

I am writing to you in His Precious Blood, with the desire to see you a firm pillar which never trembles, except before God, not fearing and not refusing any of the pains that must be borne in the Mystical Body of Holy Church, the sweet Spouse of Christ.

The soul must not be deterred by the difficulties it meets in prayer

especially when it is exhausting itself in the service of Christ's Spouse. Everything we do for her is so meritorious and so pleasing to God that our minds cannot understand and imagine it.

I recall, gentlest Father, a servant of God to whom it was revealed how pleasing whatever we do for the Church is to God; and I say this to you so that you may be encouraged to suffer for her. I know that on one of several occasions this servant of God ardently desired to give her blood, to destroy and consume everything in her for the Spouse of Christ, for Holy Church. She applied her mind to understanding her own nothingness and God's goodness to her, and she saw that out of love God had given her existence and all the graces, all the gifts which He had added thereto. When she saw and appreciated this love, this abyss of charity, she perceived that there was no means of thanking God except by loving Him. But since she could not be of any service to Him, she could not prove her love, and so she sought to see if she could find something to love for His sake, something through which she could show her love. Wherefore she saw that God loved His rational creatures exceedingly and that the love which she found in herself was present in all men, because we are all loved by God. Thus she had a means of showing whether or not she loved God because in that way she was able to be of service to Him. Then she devoted herself ardently to love of the neighbor and felt such love for his salvation that she would joyfully have given her life to obtain it. What she could not do for God she desired to do for her neighbor; and she saw that we must thank God by means of our neighbor and thus return Him love for love. Just as God, by means of His Son, the Word, has shown His love and mercy, so she wished, by her desire for the salvation of souls, to give glory to

God and to be pleasing to Him by working for her neighbor. She was seeking to know in which garden and at which table she could satisfy her hunger.

Then our Savior appeared to her and said: "Beloved daughter, you can do so in the garden of My Spouse and at the table of the most holy cross by your pain, by the anguish of desire, by vigils and prayers, and by active, persevering efforts. Learn that you cannot desire anything for the salvation of souls which you do not desire for Holy Church, because she is the universal body of all those who share in the light of holy faith, and no one can have life if he is not obedient to My Spouse. Therefore, you must desire to see your neighbors—Christians, unbelievers and all rational creatures—eating in this garden under the yoke of holy obedience and clothing themselves in the light of a living faith—that is, in good and holy works, because faith without works is dead. That is the desire and the general need of the universal body of the Church. But now, I tell you, I want you to feel a desire and a particular hunger and to be ready, if necessary, to give your life for the Mystical Body of Holy Church, for the reform of My Spouse, because upon this reform depends the good of the whole world. Why? Because darkness, ignorance, self-love, impurity and the excesses of pride have produced and are still producing night and death in the souls of the faithful. I therefore invite you and My other servants to consume yourselves in desires, vigils, prayers and other exercises, according to the dispositions that I give you, because this labor for the good of the Church is so pleasing to Me that it is rewarded not only in My servants, who have an upright, holy intention, but also in those who serve the world and who often support the Church out of self-interest and sometimes even out of respect. Thus I tell you that no one will serve her respectfully without being recompensed for it, so great is My regard for her. Yes, such a one will not fall into eternal death like those who offend and attack My Spouse, and whose outrages I shall always punish in one way or another."

Then the soul, seeing such greatness and depth in God's goodness and perceiving what it should do to please Him still more, increased more and more the ardor of its desire. It seemed to the soul that if it had been able to give its life a thousand times over each day until the Last Judgment, it would have been less than a drop of wine in the sea—which is indeed only the truth. Therefore, I invite you to work for the Church as you have always done, to be a pillar set to help and uphold this Spouse; that is your task, as I have told you. Never be shaken, either in consolation or tribulation. Many are the contrary winds that blow against those who follow the way of truth, but we should never for any reason turn our heads to look back. That is why I have told you that I wished to see you as a firm pillar. Take courage, then, dearest, sweetest Father, because this is the time to glorify God in His Spouse and to wear yourself out for her.

(Letter 282, to Niccolò da Osimo.)

Catherine's insistence on the need to support and encourage the servants of the Church went on increasing in proportion to the evils that were then besieging the Spouse of Christ, especially when the schism broke out. She wrote to Raymond: "Consider the great needs of Holy Church, alone and abandoned in everything" (Letter 372). She was to repeat this cry on her deathbed.

The first requisite for working on behalf of the Church is that we be inspired by love, without which we can understand nothing about the Church: "She is founded on love, and is herself love" (Letter 371, to Raymond of Capua). Catherine wished to receive from Christ Himself in Communion His own love of the Church, as is evident from the prayer she uttered during an ecstasy while making her thanksgiving after Communion on February 18, 1379:

As You give Yourself to me in the Communion of the Body and Blood of Your beloved Son, in which You give Yourself, God and man, whole and entire, so I beg You, O Ineffable Love, to allow me to share likewise in the Mystical Body of Holy Church, my mother,

195

and in the universal body of the Christian religion. For the fire of Your charity has made me appreciate the extent to which You wish the soul to delight in this food.

(Prayer 5.)

The second condition for working on behalf of the Church is that our love for her must feed on death to self, for what could the Church do with soldiers who were fearful and concerned only with sparing themselves in the service of the Redemption? In a letter to Blessed Raymond, Catherine wrote in the name of God:

"If he desires My glory in Holy Church, tell him that he must love sufferings and be willing to bear them with true patience. That is the way in which I shall know that he and My other servants truly seek My glory."

(Letter 272.)

She felt this so keenly that she took up the subject again in another letter to Raymond which, in fact, was her last testament, so to speak:

Cast far from you all tenderness toward yourself and all servile fear, because the Church does not need such people but rather those who are cruel to themselves and compassionate to her. That is my advice.

(Letter 373.)

Fidelity to the Church is also marked by obedience. When Raymond decided not to proceed on a mission lest he fall into the hands of the schismatics, Catherine regarded his action as an evasion that showed a lack of courage but, most of all, she saw it as a failure in obedience, and her advice to him indicated that she and he were especially bound in obedience to the service of the papacy in the person of Urban VI:

196

We are offered like dead men in the garden of Holy Church to the owner of the garden, who is "Christ on earth." Let us act, then, like dead men. A dead man neither sees nor hears nor feels. Try to kill yourself with the sword of hate and love; try to kill yourself so that you will no longer notice the injuries, outrages and reproaches of the persecutors of Holy Church, and so that you will no longer see the impossibility of your task or the probable trials. Instead, in the light of faith, see that you can do everything in Christ and that God never lays on us a burden that is too great for our strength. Even under heavy burdens we should rejoice because we then receive the gift of strength. Love of trials banishes our awareness of pain. Thus, completely dead, we shall find our food in this garden. How happy my soul will then be!

(Letter 344, to Raymond of Capua.)

Finally, loving the Church means loving its unity; but it also means understanding the riches and breadth of this unity. Our viewpoint must be as all-encompassing as God's and we should have that sense of the Church which enables us to love and understand vocations other than our own. On the one hand, the gift that each one of us receives puts him at the service of others and binds him to them. As God explained to Catherine:

"I could easily have endowed each one with everything that he needs spiritually and materially, but I have willed that each one have need of the other and that they thus become My ministers charged with distributing the graces and gifts which they have received from Me. Man cannot avoid being compelled to practice charity, whether he wishes it or not. Nevertheless, his actions will not merit him any grace if they are not done for love of Me. You see, then, so that charity will be practiced by men, I have made them My ministers and have given them various situations and stations in life. That proves to you that in My house there are many mansions and that I want nothing but love."

(Dialogue, Chap. 7.)

197

On the other hand, fraternal charity necessarily makes us understand that our fellow men are different from us and causes us to rejoice in their welfare: "Rejoice in everything you see, saying 'Thanks be to You, O Eternal Father, who in Your house have many mansions'" (Letter 64, to William of England).

But why go on trying vainly to list all the elements in true love of the Church when loving the Spouse of Christ as she should be loved means loving her as Christ does?

24. Reform of the Church

❖❖❖❖❖❖❖❖❖

WE HAVE seen, then, what love of the Church means. The ardent, unremitting desire for renewal and reform that animated Catherine's whole life was fully in this tradition. Her zeal for reform was not opposition to superiors or egocentric aggressiveness; it was not born of any abstract theories nor did it lead to any strange course of action. Instead she was inspired by her love of God and her will to give Him glory; her only aim was to spread love and reform souls, and her motive was never pride or censorious judgment, but rather love and service, working in union with God and in close dependence on Him.

There is no lack of evidence in her writings that this was indeed her attitude; in fact, the only difficulty is to select the most expressive texts. We may sometimes smile at the way she expresses herself, yet her spontaneous reactions clearly reveal the secrets of her heart:

What tongue can relate the marvels of God? Not mine, poor miserable creature that I am. Therefore, I wish to keep silence and concern myself solely with God's glory, the salvation of souls, the renewal and exaltation of Holy Church, and, with the grace and strength of the Holy Spirit, to persevere unto death. This desire

199

drives and will drive me to cry with great love and compassion to our "Christ on earth" and to you, Father, and to all my dear sons. I asked and obtained your petition. Therefore, rejoice, rejoice and be glad!

O God, sweet Love, hasten to fulfil the desires of Your servants!

I do not wish to say more about it, and I have really said nothing. I am in anguish and am dying with desire. Have mercy on me! Ask the Divine Goodness and "Christ on earth" to make a clean sweep and that quickly!

(Letter 219, to Raymond of Capua.)

Her own words explain what the exaltation of the Church meant to her—a sanctity completely in accordance with the Gospel and a wholehearted enthusiasm for the salvation of the entire world. She also repeats God's own explanation of the providential role played by the persecutions which He permits:

In particular, He explained to me very clearly and familiarly the mystery of the present persecution of Holy Church, as well as her future renewal and exaltation; and He assured me that He permits the present trials in order to lead her back to her original condition. The Sovereign Sweet Truth recalled the words of the holy Gospel—that it must needs be that scandal come into the world, but woe to him through whom the scandal comes. He meant to say, "I permit this time of persecution in order to free My Spouse from the thorns that surround her on all sides; but I do not permit men's evil intentions. Do you know what I am doing? What I did before when, with a whip of cords, I drove the buyers and sellers from the Temple because I was angered at their turning the house of God into a den of thieves. So today I am making a whip of cords out of creatures and, with this whip, I am driving out the unclean, greedy, avaricious and proud merchants that are trafficking in the gifts of the Holy Ghost." So, with the whip of persecution by creatures, He drove them out and, by dint of persecutions and tribulations, He turned them from their lawless, shameful ways.

The fire of love increased in me and I was amazed because I saw Christians and unbelievers entering the side of Christ crucified. The desire and ardor of love made me go with them and enter Christ, sweet Jesus, in the company of St. Dominic, the one and only John [probably her affectionate nickname for Raymond], and all my sons.

(Letter 219, to Raymond of Capua.)

Because of her ardent love, Catherine was at peace and secure even when she feared that she had displeased the Pope:

Most Holy Father, in the light of reason and truth examine the cause of your displeasure with me and do not punish me for it, because it is enough that you are displeased. To whom shall I go if you abandon me? Who shall save me? Who shall be my refuge if you turn me away? When persecutors pursue me, I take shelter with you and with the other children and servants of God. If, displeased and indignant with me, you abandon me, I shall hide in the wounds of Christ crucified, whose Vicar you are. I know that He will receive me because He does not will the death of the sinner. And when I have been welcomed by Him, you will not drive me away any more; instead we both shall remain at our posts to fight manfully with the weapons of virtue on the side of Christ's sweet Spouse. That is where I want to end my life in tears, sweat and sighs, giving my blood and the marrow of my bones. And if the whole world drove me off, I should not be disturbed but, in tears and unruffled patience, I should rest on the bosom of the sweet Spouse.

(Letter 276, to Raymond of Capua, in reference to Urban VI.)

Her humility is very evident in her keen sense of personal responsibility for the sins of the world. She never lost sight

201

of this responsibility and was unable to think of the renewal of the Church without acknowledging her own sins and making an effort to reform herself:

If I loved Him truly, my fidelity would go so far as to make me die a thousand times a day, if that were necessary and possible, for the glory and praise of His name. I would have confidence that God would become my protector and defense as He was to the glorious martyrs who ran joyfully to torture. If I were faithful, I would fear nothing and would be certain that God is for me what He was for them. Surely His power has not grown weak! Cannot He provide for my needs? I do not truly trust Him because I do not love Him. The fear I feel proves the tepidity of my love. The light of faith in my soul is darkened by my infidelities to my Creator and by my reliance on self. I confess and cannot deny that the root is not yet pulled out of my soul and that it is the obstacle to the works that God wishes to do in me and to those which He wishes me to do, works which are therefore powerless to attain the glorious and useful end proposed by Him.

Alas, alas, my Lord! Woe is me, a miserable wretch! Am I then going to remain like this always and everywhere and in everything? Will my unfaithfulness continue to bar the way of Your Providence? It will certainly do so if Your mercy does not destroy me in order to remake me again. Destroy me, then, Lord; break the hardness of my heart. I do not wish to be any longer an obstacle to Your operations.

(Letter 344, to Raymond of Capua.)

To Catherine, any renewal meant an immolation and gift of herself, a love that united her to others and that derived its ideal and its strength from Christ. This was not a projection of her ego—which modern psychologists recognize so well—but the humble submission of herself to the loving, demanding action of the Holy Spirit, whose aim was to revive the beauty and youth of the Spouse of Christ.

It has pleased God that His kingdom should be a field in which wheat is sown by His love and cockle by "the enemy," His intention being to lead His followers to a purer faith and a truer love. But, alas, sin in the Church often becomes an occasion for scandal and alienation for those very people who commit the same sins in secret. Again, we can react to evil in a way that puts us on the very same level with it. "He who pursues, follows," said Nietzsche about virtuous souls that judge others harshly.

Because of the cockle, there have always been reform movements in the Church, some of which are on the divine plane because they are inspired by God, while others never rise above the human level because they are tainted with the spirit of criticism or self-righteousness. This was true of Catherine's time: for some of the contemporary "spiritual" souls, a fervent reaction against the surrounding corruption became a flight, an escape into mysticism, or else it turned into a prophetical tendency, judging, condemning and hurling anathemas. But far from withdrawing from the Church because of the sins she saw in it, Catherine immersed herself more deeply in it and died for it.

Divinely enlightened, she continued to see "the face of the Church" befouled and disfigured by leprosy caused by the sins of Christians, particularly the clergy. But God's intention in granting her this insight was to urge her on to a greater love, more fervent prayer, more ardent, generous and effective desires to renew the Church. Accordingly, this inner light continued to show her that the priestly office remains unalterably holy because of the Blood which it transmits, and that the guilt of the man who betrays his priesthood is undiminished. One of the failings against which the Lord took care to put her on her guard was the tendency to judge and to set oneself up as an arbiter of sin. At the same time, He showed her the refuge against this evil: "Your refuge lies in giving honor and glory to My name and in ensuring that the incense of continual prayer ascends to Me for these unfortunate souls. . . . Your shelter must be Christ crucified" (*Dialogue*, Chap. 124).

Christ makes His followers see the sins of the world in order to increase their love and inspire them with more ardent courage to work at their tasks, while others look at sin through their own eyes and consequently draw apart by themselves.

Perhaps the best test of an apostle's spirit is his reaction when confronted with sin, particularly the sin of people in responsible positions. Does he become more humble, more zealous, less inclined to judge and more resolved to act? As a result of his experience does he love the unity and universality of the Church more?

In the Church, whose mission is to save sinners, a fervent apostle must learn from Christ to look sin in the face and conquer it by loving the sinner and offering himself for his salvation.

At first glance, we may be tempted to think that there is not much to learn from what Catherine writes about the reform of the Church and the sins of the unworthy clergy of her day. However, a little reflection will show us that while, with God's grace, the situation is incomparably improved today, Catherine still has a basic lesson to teach us. She can still show us that, in order to imitate Christ and cooperate in His work, we must break more completely with all that offends God, have a more sincere love for the sinner, no matter who he may be—even a Pharisee—and an efficacious will to work for his salvation by prayer or action. For that is the way in which we nourish ourselves at the table of the holy cross.

Catherine's descriptions of the Church as "livid, disfigured or leprous" always grate on us a little when we recall the love of Christ that makes His Spouse "holy, without spot or stain," and we would rather speak about the sick *members* of the Church—the Christian society of such and such an age, the clergy of such and such a century or country, and so on. Holy Church certainly has sinful members, and heretics or schismatics can be scandalized by them, turn away from the Church and call themselves pure or spiritual in contrast. But the true Church, who is the mother of souls, never ceases to proclaim that sinners are still her children and that they remain members of her Mystical Body (unless they have voluntarily separated themselves from her by apostasy or have been cut off from her by excommunication). Even in the face of Nazi persecution, Pius XI emphasized this doctrine, and Pius XII expounded it with precision in his great encyclical *Mystici Corporis.*

This disposition of Providence serves the mercy of the Redeemer, who thus cures the sick members within His own Body; it shows His wisdom, for the means of salvation do not derive their value from the human instruments who apply them but from Him alone. Nor should we be surprised at this, because the Gospel parable warns us that the kingdom of heaven is like a field in which the Father has sown wheat and His enemy cockle.

25. The Priesthood

CATHERINE'S great and burning love for the Spouse of Christ gave her ever keener insight into the role played by priests. She saw that the reform of the clergy was the remedy for the excruciating evils of the world, and her prayers are evidence of her profound conviction and longing: "You gave us the light of the Apostles when it was needed. Now, today, when we have even greater need for light, raise up another St. Paul to enlighten the whole world" (Prayer 8). With the needs of the Church in mind, she prayed:

I beg You to turn toward Yourself once more the hearts and wills of the ministers of Holy Church, Your Spouse. May they serve You, the immolated Lamb, poor, humble and meek, by following the path of the most holy cross and in Your way, not theirs.

(Prayer 2.)

She regarded the reform of the Church and the salvation of the whole world as one and the same thing, as is clear from a letter to Blessed Raymond in which she explained the main ideas of the *Dialogue*: "Although these words promised the salvation of the whole world, nevertheless the servant of God extended her prayer and asked especially for the salvation of the world" (Letter 272). She understood prophetically the role that priests play in the Church; and she knew that when she saw the Spouse disfigured and appearing like a leper, it was because an unworthy clergy, who instead of giving filial service to the Church, sought to satisfy their basest passions at her expense. She foresaw that the great schism which was to rend the Christian world would be "the sin of the clerics." But she saw, too, that the Church would be restored to the world when there were pastors worthy of their office, for she was also acutely aware of the great dignity of the priesthood. Her own words express her conviction better than any commentary we could make:

The ministers whom the Sovereign Goodness has chosen as His Christs must especially be angels and not men; and they are truly so if they do not deprive themselves of the light, for they really exercise the function of angels. The angels serve each man in the way God has laid down for them; they are the guardians whom His goodness has given us. In the same way, priests are put in the Mystical Body of Holy Church to distribute the Body and Blood of Jesus crucified, wholly God and wholly man by the union of the Divine Nature with human nature.

(Letter 2, to Fr. Andrea de' Vitroni.)

But, as she well knew, the dignity of the priesthood must be accompanied by true sanctity. Therefore, when writing to a certain worldly prelate, she prayerfully exhorted him to lead a life worthy of his priesthood:

Such a one does not nourish himself at the table of a fervent desire for God and the salvation of souls. God nevertheless demands that we all take this nourishment there, but He especially demands it of the pastors of Holy Church, to whom He has confided the care of souls. They must be true shepherds, like the holy Good Shepherd, who

offered and gave His life for His sheep, and who, by the sacrifice of
the cross, has accomplished obedience to His Father and our salvation. He never refused toil and fatigue; never was His desire for our
salvation lessened either by the devil or by the Jews who cried:
"Come down from the cross!" or by our ingratitude. And we must
follow in His footsteps. That is what I invite you to do, dearest
Father. Recently, God has placed you in the garden of Holy Church.
He has given you the care of souls so that you may do as the holy,
gentle shepherds did when, in times gone by, the Church of God
abounded in virtuous men who contemplated truth in the light of
their minds. They took Jesus crucified as their model. In the light
[of faith] they knew the hunger that the sweet Word has for our
salvation, and they loved Him so much that suffering and giving their
lives were a great joy to them. Their friends were the poor; their
riches were the love of God, the salvation of their sheep and the
exaltation of Holy Church. They never ceased to offer ardent, tender
desires to God, and they taught the doctrines of the Faith by the
example of a good and holy life. When their power grew, they did
not feel proud because of it but only humbled themselves the more
profoundly because the light which they possessed made them bow
their heads at the sight of the burden and responsibility laid on them
by the care of souls. . . . I wish you not to permit any lessening
of the holy desire that you have, and ought to have, of meeting the
obligations of your office.

(Letter 341, to Bishop-elect Angelo.)

Elsewhere she described admirably those priests whose
lives are worthy of the dignity of their office:

"There is no greater dignity in this life. They are My anointed:
I call them My 'Christs' because I have given them the office of
administering Me to you." (*Dialogue,* Chap. 113.)
"These ministers resemble the sun: clothed and filled with Me,
the true Sun, they act like the sun, which warms and illuminates
and by its heat makes the earth bear fruit. In the same way,
these dear ministers of mine have been elected, anointed and

placed in the Mystical Body of Holy Church to administer Me, the Sun, that is, the Body and Blood of My only-begotten Son, with the other sacraments which draw life from the Blood; and they administer It actually and spiritually, namely, by radiating light in the Mystical Body of Holy Church—the light of supernatural knowledge and the color of a virtuous, holy life, that is, by following the teaching of My sweet Truth and by giving forth the heat of ardent charity. By thus spreading warmth and by illuminating sterile souls with the light of knowledge, they make them bud forth. By their holy, well-regulated lives, they put to flight the darkness of mortal sin and infidelity and set to rights the lives of those who live in the dark disorder of sin or in the cold privation of grace. You see, then, that they are suns; and, thanks to Me, they act like suns since by their love they are one with Me and I with them." (*Ibid.*, Chap. 119.)

Hence St. Catherine truly regarded God's priests as "other Christs called to conquer death and to restore the world to life."

In the fourteenth century, the most casual observer could see the flaunted luxury and corruption of an ignorant, debased clergy, ruled by worldly ambition and over-submissive to the temporal powers. However, thanks be to God, since the reforms instituted by the Council of Trent we can scarcely even imagine priests such as these, without vocation or priestly spirit. In Catherine's case, God Himself supernaturally enlightened her soul to make her understand the abysmal wretchedness existing in His Church:

O ineffable Love! You show us the needs of the world, and particularly those of Holy Church. . . . Therefore, I shall look at myself in You in order to purify myself there and, after having thus purified myself, I shall cry out in the presence of Your mercy, begging You to cast the eyes of Your pity upon the distress of Your Spouse. (Prayer 24.)

"My sweet daughter, see how the face of My Spouse is besmirched with impurity and self-love and swollen with the pride and avarice of those who are nourished at her breast! But take your tears and sweat, draw them from the fountain of My divine love, and wash her face."

(Letter 222, to Raymond of Capua.)

Unable to contain herself, she allowed her anguish to pour out in a letter to a prelate:

Open your eyes and see the mortal wounds that ravage the world in general and the Mystical Body of Holy Church in particular. Alas, my heart is breaking at seeing so many outrages committed against God. See how the infernal wolf carries off the young sheep that are grazing in the garden of Holy Church, and there is no one to snatch them from his jaws. The shepherds are asleep in their self-love, avarice and pleasures. . . . Ah, do not be silent any longer but cry out as if you had a hundred thousand voices. . . . The Spouse of Christ is as pale as death, for she has lost her blood, the Blood of Christ. . . . They are robbing her through pride when they take for themselves the glory that belongs to God; they are robbing her through simony by selling the gifts and grace that were given us free at the cost of the Blood of the Son of God. Alas, I am dying and yet I cannot die!

(Letter 16, to a great prelate.)

Enlightened by God as she was, her condemnation of the unworthy clergy of her day was indeed a terrible one: "They are devils incarnate," and we know what depths of decadence, horror and baseness this term held for the Saint.

Yet she never lost sight of the pre-eminent dignity of the priesthood. Even when she was voicing the most cutting rebukes and uttering the most poignant cries of sorrow for the evil lives of the clergy, her spirit of faith and her filial respect for the priestly office did not desert her.

210

"You must have great respect for them since, because of their virtues, they are My beloved sons, and by their virtues, the suns of the Mystical Body of Holy Church. But if every virtuous man is worthy of love, then these are even more worthy because of the ministry which I have entrusted to them. You must love them because of the virtue and dignity of the sacrament, and you must detest the sins of those who live evil lives. Nevertheless, you must not set yourself up as their judges. I do not wish that, because they are My 'Christs' and you must love and respect the authority that I have confided to them.

"You know that if a filthy, badly dressed man came to you bringing you a treasure that would give you life, then out of love for the treasure and the prince who sent it to you, you would be very careful not to despise the bearer because of his rags and filth. Of course, he would be repellent to you; but, out of love for his master, you would devise some means of getting him to wash himself and change his clothing. That is how you must act if you are to be charitable; that is the way I wish to see you conduct yourself toward those of My ministers who, in their squalid garments of vice, all torn with lack of charity, bring you those great treasures, the sacraments of Holy Church. No matter what the sins of the ministers may be, you obtain the life of grace when you receive these sacraments worthily, out of love for Me, the eternal God, who sends them to you, and out of love for the life of grace that you receive from this treasure, the whole God and the whole man, that is, from the Body and Blood of My Son united to My divine nature. You must detest, you must hate their sins and apply yourself, by charity and prayers, to re-clothing them, to washing their uncleanness with your tears and your great desire to see Me dress them in the garment of charity."

(*Dialogue*, Chap. 120.)

What exactly was Catherine's conception of the priest and his office? We can easily find out from her *Dialogue* and letters. Thus to Cardinal Peter of Ostia she wrote:

I wish you to busy yourself with nothing except the glory of God, saving souls and serving the sweet Spouse of Christ. . . . You know that the divine goodness has placed you in the Mystical Body of Holy Church, nursing you at the breast of the sweet Spouse only so that you may eat, at the table of the holy cross, the food of the glory of God and the salvation of souls.

(Letter 11.)

This was the spirit in which Catherine prayed and sacrificed herself for the reform of the clergy.

26. "Christ on Earth"

❖❖❖❖❖❖❖❖❖

IT IS impossible to speak about St. Catherine of Siena without mentioning her grasp of the meaning of the Papacy. Indeed she is often remembered mainly for her remonstrating with the Pope and for her special name for him—"Christ on earth."

She did not pause to examine the idea of the Church or the parish or even the diocese, for she was not a theologian writing a thesis on the Church and the hierarchy. Nor was she a reformer devising a plan of action. She was, rather, a mystic contemplating the mystery of the Church in the divine light, a mystic whose prayer was for all men, an apostle doing all the good that was in her power.

She never did set out to explain the full meaning of the expression she habitually used when speaking of the Pope— "Christ on earth"—yet her acute awareness of the defects of the two Popes with whom she had dealings and to whom she described the condition of the Church, is clear evidence that she drew a sharp distinction between the office and the man. She regarded the Pope as the Vicar whom Christ left on earth when He ascended to heaven:

When You departed from us, You did not leave us orphans; You gave

213

us Your Vicar, who administers to us the baptism of the Holy Spirit, and not only once, as in the baptism by water in which we are washed once and for all, but he continually purifies us by holy penance and blots out our sins.

(Prayer 3.)

Occasionally, she regarded the Pope as a sign of Christ's love for His Spouse, just as the liturgy refers to the bishop as the "bridegroom of the Church." But, more frequently, her thoughts turned to the keys which Christ gave to Peter, and she liked to remark that the Pope "has the keys of the wine cellar," in which the fruits of the Blood are kept, a metaphor which she developed at great length in her *Dialogue*:

> "To whom did He leave the keys of His Blood? To the glorious Apostle Peter, to those who have taken his place, and to those who shall succeed him until the Day of Judgment. All have or will have the same power as Peter. None of their defects can lessen this power or render less perfect the Blood and any of the sacraments. . . . Therefore 'Christ on earth' retains the keys of the Blood. . . . If you remember, I used an allegory to explain what I mean: the Mystical Body of Holy Church is the wine cellar in which the Blood of My only-begotten Son is kept. From this Blood all the sacraments draw their powers, and they have no life or power except through the Blood. At the door of this wine cellar stands 'Christ on earth,' whom I Myself have commissioned to dispense the Blood. It is his right and duty to choose his ministers so that they may help him in distributing the Blood to the Christian world. Only those who are approved by, and united with, him become his ministers, and no others. From him comes every clerical office. From him each one receives the office of dispensing this glorious Blood. Just as he has chosen them to be his aides, so too it is his duty to reprimand them, and that is the way I wish it to be."

(*Dialogue*, Chap. 115.)

But she did not forget that the priestly office is not part of the man, as we see from the letter she wrote to Bernabò Visconti even before the Florentine war broke out:

Although he were a devil incarnate, I should not oppose him but should always humble myself and ask for the Blood out of mercy, because that is the only way you can obtain and benefit by It. . . . Enough, therefore, father: I wish that we humbly place our foreheads on the knees of Christ in heaven with affection and love, and upon those of "Christ on earth," who takes His place, out of respect for the precious Blood, of which he holds the keys. It is open to those to whom he opens It; It is closed to those against whom he closes It. He has the power, the authority; and no one can take them from him because they have been confided to him by the Sweet Supreme Truth.

(Letter 28.)

That is why she denounced so strongly the catastrophe of the schism and trembled for those who were in any way responsible for it: "I can tell you that he who is not for the truth is against the truth" (Letter 310, to three Italian Cardinals).

Any defects displayed by the Popes only increase our duty of praying for them. At the very moment when Urban VI's shortcomings were the occasion of such great danger to the Church, our Lord gave Catherine light on the duty of the cardinals—and anyone who has to work with ecclesiastical superiors of whatever rank can profit by what she learned:

"Tell all the pillars of the Church that, if they want to rebuild the devastated ruins, they must be united and be like a cloak that covers the faults of their Father. Let them live a regular life; let them fear Me and love Me; let them march all together, forgetting themselves. If they do this, I who am the Light will give them the light necessary for Holy Church. Now that they see what they must do together, let them propose it promptly and boldly to My Vicar, who will then not be able to resist their just demands, because his intentions are good and holy."

(Letter 371, to Raymond of Capua.)

When we read the remonstrations which Catherine wrote in her letters to the Popes, we must not take them out of the historical context in which they were dictated. In the Middle Ages, human relations were much simpler and more direct, in a world that was much less complex than ours. As we have already remarked, a reputation for sanctity apparently gave the one who possessed it an almost official role. However, Gregory XI was too much the great lord and was too intelligent to be easily swayed; moreover, he was able to communicate with Catherine only through an interpreter. But in the case of Urban VI, it was different. Catherine had come to know him fairly well before his election, on the occasion of her journey to Avignon, and she had had conversations with him about perfection and reform. She did not wish to oppose his authority but only to serve it:

Your authority extends to everything, but your view is limited, just as any ordinary man's is, and so it is necessary that your children, in the sincerity of their hearts and without any servile fear, should see and do whatever is useful for the glory of God, for your salvation and the salvation of the sheep that are in your care. I know that Your Holiness ardently desires to have helpers who can serve him, but, if they are to do so, you must listen patiently to them.

(Letter 302, to Urban VI.)

That is why, in her ecstasies after Communion, she often prayed for the Vicar of Christ, asking that he be given sanctity: "Open the eyes of Your Vicar on this earth. Bring it about that he may not love You for his own sake or love himself for his own sake, but make him love You for Yourself, and himself for You alone " (Prayer 1).

There were no sufferings which she was not ready to bear, before God, for the Holy Father because of the commission that had been given him by Christ, whose place he took on earth. She had seen the depths of evil to which men can descend; she knew Urban VI's shortcomings despite his good intentions, yet she did not lose sight of the office that had been conferred on him. He was still "Christ on earth."

27. Self-Sacrifice for the Church

❖❖❖❖❖❖❖❖

WE COME now to Catherine's deepest and most closely kept secret, the very heart of apostolic sanctity, which is the offering of self for the Church, an act so great that it surpasses and enlarges all the soul's activities, so pure and so genuine that it overcomes all obstacles and makes up for all deficiencies. Therefore, we must first of all try to understand what it meant to her, after which we shall meditate on her great secret as she confided it to Raymond, her closest friend.

Our reflections in the preceding chapters on her love of the Church, her zeal for its renewal, the awareness of the significance of the priesthood and the Papacy, have allowed us some insight into the mystery of the close relationship that existed between Christ and her whom He had chosen as His colleague in His work. Yet we feel that we are still only on the threshold of the mystery. Fortunately, however, Christ, who makes His mystics witnesses to His bountiful love in its various activities, has willed to tell us more about the mystery and to teach us the extent to which the Church is one with Him.

In a prayer which we quoted above, Catherine asked to be allowed to enter into communion with the Mystical Body as she had just become one with Christ in the Blessed Sacrament. This prayer will give us some access, through words and formulas, to the Saint's most exalted experiences, for she was a witness to the love of Christ in His Church, not only because she repeated what she learned in the secret communications of love but also because she expressed it in her life. We catch a glimpse of what she meant by phrases such as "pouring herself out drop by drop into the Church" or, if you will, causing her life to pass into the Church. In another figure of speech more extraordinary still, and which we have already mentioned, she tells how she felt her heart being squeezed like a sponge to wash the face of the Spouse defiled by the sin of men, particularly of the very ministers of the Church itself. This should not surprise us, because the words of the mystics are often disconcerting since they refer to experiences that are incommunicably personal. Again, the mystics themselves never cease to lament the inadequacy, inaccuracy and pitiable poverty of the human language they are forced to use in trying to describe what they have seen and heard.

Two rather different but converging texts from St. Catherine show us that pouring out oneself into the Church through love means being united with that which is essential in the Church and which, consequently, is found both in the Church triumphant and in the Church militant, where one and the same charity aspires to the glory of God in the full realization of His plans, here below through pain and by blissful repose in eternity. Is that what St. Paul meant when (see Eph. 3:10) he spoke about "the manifold wisdom of God" being "made known to the Principalities and the Powers in the heavens" through the Church?

In a letter which modern critics date April 1378,[1] Cath-

---

[1] Since this letter was formerly thought to be the second of those which the Saint

erine speaks about three stops or halts which she made while in ecstasy: the first in hell, the second with Christ-on-earth, and the third with the inhabitants of heaven; or, as we would perhaps say, with the *guilty* Church, where Catherine saw the sins and responsibilities of the Church; with the Church *militant*, where she shared in the aspirations of the best elements in the Church (aspirations to sanctity and apostolic effort), and with the Church *triumphant*, where desire becomes joy and repose. The following quotation from her letter, even though it is obscure, is necessary to show her train of thought:

He so filled me with joy that the very members of my body felt as if they were melting and dissolving like wax in a fire. My soul then made three dwelling places: with the devils, through knowledge of myself. . . . To complete my happiness, He caused me to dwell with "Christ on earth" . . . and to walk and talk with those who truly taste God and with the family of "Christ on earth." . . . And, wonderful to relate, instead of being mutually exclusive, these three dwellings did not interfere with, but rather enhanced, each other.

(Letter 226.)

In her last letter to Raymond, which, as we have said, was actually her testament, she wished to confide in him as much as possible and tried to describe what had taken place within her after she had heard "most captivating words" from the

---

wrote to Raymond, it was naturally regarded as having been composed during the period when he was in Avignon. But the references to "the triumph of our Archbishop" and to "the family of 'Christ on earth' " suggest that it should be dated during the spring of 1378, at the time when Catherine had just learned the news of the election of "our Archbishop," as she called him. The mention of "the family" would seem to indicate that a whole group of people who longed for reform had wanted, if not prepared for, the election of Urban VI, whose violence, however, even before the obduracy of advancing years set in, frustrated his excellent intentions to make reforms. The difference of opinion about the date of the letter involves a divergence of but two years, between the spring of 1376 and that of 1378, and, so far as we are concerned here, has no bearing on the profound thoughts expressed in the letter.

Sovereign Truth Himself, words which she did not dare repeat. She endeavored to explain to Raymond the mysteries that had been accomplished in her and that undoubtedly were going to lead her to a definitive union with God. She showed him that she was united with the saints in heaven and freed from the earth, but also that she did not wish to, and could not, partake in the delights of their love but only in the infinite hunger which they knew during the course of their mortal lives and which they still felt. Here we are at the heart of the Church, the heart that is love and that gives life to the whole Mystical Body by being united to it and by spending itself for it:

Desire for Him becomes so much a part of one that the memory retains nothing but Him and the will can desire only Him. And not only does the soul refuse the things of earth but even when it is in the midst of those who live in the true city, [that is, the blessed in heaven], it cannot and does not wish to rejoice in their joy but only in the hunger which they feel now and which they felt when they were pilgrims and wayfarers on this earth.

(Letter 373, to Raymond of Capua.)

The offering of self to God for His Church will therefore necessarily mean being united with all the love that is given to save men and incorporate them with Him; or, better still, it is charity assuming its true dimensions in the soul, which then goes beyond self to unite itself with God, allowing Him to live in it to the full extent of His love. We shall understand this better presently.

First of all, truth demands that we confront the mystery of self-immolation for the Church, not as we think it is or as we have experienced it ourselves and much less as it appears in human achievements, but as it is in God's truth. (At this point we should re-read the first chapter of the Epistle to the

221

Ephesians.) As for Catherine, she saw it in a direct light whose nature we cannot know, and immediately the contrast between the ideal and the reality burst upon her, becoming for her an unbearable agony. What was, in fact, this Spouse beloved by Christ? What had men, particularly those in the most responsible positions, made of it? The Church was torn asunder by schism, by a schism caused by the cardinals themselves. This was, indeed, a sorrowful period in the life of the Spouse.

For Catherine, the offering of herself took the form of a question, an anxious inquiry: "What is to be done? What can I do?" God's answer brought before her again her personal mission and task in the Church:

> "Once more offer your life and never give yourself any rest. I have prepared you for this ministry, you and all those who follow and will follow you. Therefore, always apply yourselves to increasing your desires and never let them grow less."
>
> (Letter 371, to Raymond of Capua.)

We should keep in mind this idea of desires that must be expanded so as to reach the proportions of God's intention. Too often, when we speak of offering oneself, we imagine a passivity ready to undergo trials and bear with difficulties rather than undertaking bravely what the task demands. In this context, when we speak of "desires," we mean to say that offering of self must become a sharing in the love that is the substance of the Church and a dedication of our lives to laboring willingly and as effectively as possible. The period in which Catherine lived was no time for her or her companions to wrap themselves up in idle defeatism. Everywhere they looked, there was chaos; in fact, never before had matters in the Church seemed so hopeless: in Avignon there was an antipope surrounded by cardinals and supported by the

222

greatest powers of the day, while in Rome itself the populace was so dissatisfied that it was ready to attack the legitimate successor of St. Peter. This surely was not a time to become discouraged; it was instead an age in which the faithful children of the Church had to enlarge their desires to the dimensions of divine love. It is true that the catholicity which Christ promised to His Church was brought about by the work, zeal and prayers of great missionaries; but it is also true that His promise to build His Church on Peter becomes a reality through the fidelity which He gives to those who must carry the weight of the Church, especially in certain hours of tragedy, the hours of "the powers of darkness." This fidelity, nevertheless, is not faced toward the past but toward the future, to that future in which the redeeming love of Christ must be poured out on humanity.

Furthermore—and this is the second essential aspect of the offering of self which we must understand thoroughly— it is not a question of sufferings or bodily death, because such things are small indeed when measured against Him who is "infinite and who wants infinite works." The Church, being herself love, can be built only in love. That is why the offering of self is the form which charity takes; and that, too, is why victory is assured to it, as Catherine implied in the words with which she concluded her testament, her most self-revealing letter to Raymond: "By the power of the fire of the divine, most ardent and inestimable charity" (Letter 371, to Raymond of Capua).

28. True Love of God

❖❖❖❖❖❖❖❖❖

IT IS now time to formulate the conclusion that follows inevitably from all we have said. Apostolic sanctity is sanctity in its essentials; it is true charity. By responding faithfully to the circumstances and demands of her day, Catherine found the essential and enduring elements in Christianity. True, her language, figures of speech and allusions are those of fourteenth-century Tuscany, but the style is her own. A daughter of the people, she was unlettered and without human culture: she learned how to read only by a miracle and, as we noted, there is serious doubt about the claim that she knew how to write, also as the result of a miracle. She dictated her writings as she spoke, and she spoke as she felt. Her experiences and her descriptions of them are very much her own, although she evidently owed much to the sermons she heard and the conversations she had, especially with Fra Raymond.

She was also greatly indebted to the influence of the "Spirituals" in particular, and it is possible to quote certain expressions of Ubertino of Casale which crept into her writings. An Augustinian influence is also perceptible in her, due no doubt to her association with the hermits of Lecceto, not far from Siena. But all that only proves what is already evident—that every Christian, even the most inspired, the most enlightened by the Holy Spirit, is only a debtor to others. This fact, which is in the province of the history of spirituality, need not concern us here. We are interested only in what Catherine did and said, in those things which, in becoming part of her, became her message to the Church.

It is even more remarkable that she was able to sift the gold from the "spiritual" current and that her grasp of what the Church means preserved her from the apocalyptic and reforming errors of her day. The evil she saw only drew her closer to the Church and caused her to proclaim the essential nature of the Mystical Body as forcefully as she did.

God is love and gives Himself to us; the cross of Christ is the manifestation of His infinite love. The Christian's duty is to make his life revolve around this fact and to love God to the point of becoming another Christ "through a union of love," just as he has become, by right, another Christ through his incorporation into the Mystical Body. This union of love unites him to everything that God loves and makes his neighbor "one with him." Hence by serving his neighbor in every manner possible, he will seek a way to repay what he owes to God.

This love, more than any other, can be achieved only by viewing things as they really are. God is He who is. Everything is made only by Him and must exist only for Him. True love, then, means loving Him for His own sake, without self-interest and solely for Himself. Knowing and doing this, the soul can discover His love, which is infinite and gratuitous. That is the secret: he who truly loves God learns the truth about the love of God. Hence, in loving the Church, his love reaches its true dimensions, being centered not on himself but on God, not remaining limited to himself but becoming universal, like God's love, and devoted to carrying out the plan that God has willed by confiding the building up of the Church to His faithful followers.

Catherine's love of Christ necessarily took the form of love for souls and the Church, because it was impossible for her to be united with Him without immediately sharing the thirst of which He died, the thirst for our salvation, to the glory of His Father. In Christ, Catherine was passionately devoted to the Person of the Son, who is one with the Father in the unity of the Spirit. She saw that He was, with all His heart, a Savior; He had an infinite desire for our salvation, but the cross of His sufferings and death was finite because it had an end and a limit: "There is no possible comparison between that which is finite and that which is infinite." The true disciple, then, shares in the infinite desire that is still present in Christ, who died from it and who now lives in glory in heaven. "God loves His creature infinitely." That is why the soul, from the moment it becomes a servant of God, loves creatures so much. It sees the love which God has for His children, and one of the conditions for love is "to love that which the beloved loves."

True love of God becomes first a contemplative gaze at Him and then generous desire and activity in the service of the neighbor. Thus, in the very act of communing with Christ and in the will to respond to His love, the soul's desire to share in His life becomes intertwined with its love of its neighbor, who is one with Him in His Mystical Body.

The soul's love of Christ must take this form no matter what the externals of its vocation may be, for things are worldly only when they are made so by being cut off from God. As Catherine has told us, a person's interior spirit is indeed fragile if he loses it simply by changing from one place to another. Such an ideal can be crucifying if one takes its demands seriously. To quote Catherine once more: "Those

who love God, not for their own sakes, but because He is
Supreme and Eternal Goodness, have little regard for their
own lives and can no longer think of themselves" (Letter 16,
to a great prelate); they have become "hungry" for souls and
"are clothed in true, sincere virtue." It is easy, then, to understand the formula which the Saint used so often: "For the
glory of God, to feed on souls at the table of the holy cross."

Index

229

A NOTE ON THE TYPE

IN WHICH THIS BOOK WAS SET

This book has been set in Weiss, an interesting face created by E. R. Weiss of Germany, who prefers to be called a painter. While he has studied almost every known letter in the world and copied inscriptions from Roman monuments, Renaissance capitals and fantastic baroque letter-forms from gravestones, he still remains a painter. The Weiss types, while traditional letters, are the product of our own time. Lines of text take on a gracious air—an easy, limpid flow when set in this modern type design. Weiss types have good color and create dignity whenever one sees them, either in a book or advertisement. This book was composed and printed by the York Composition Company, Inc., of York, and bound by Moore and Company of Baltimore. The design and typography are by Howard N. King.